THE HUMILITY OF GOD

The Humility of God

A FRANCISCAN PERSPECTIVE

ILIA DELIO, O.S.F.

franciscan
media
Cincinnati, Ohio

Excerpts from *The Jerusalem Bible*, copyright © 1966 by Darton, Longman & Todd, Ltd. and Doubleday, a division of Random House Inc. Reprinted by permission. Excerpts from *Exclusion and Embrace* by Miroslav Volf ©1996. Published by Abingdon Press. Used by permission. Excerpt from "A God Who Gets Foolishly Close," published in *America*, May 27, 2000. Reprinted with permission of America Press. Excerpts from "Christ, Word of God and Exemplar of Humanity: The Roots of Franciscan Christocentrism and Its Implications for Today," from *The Cord*. Published by the Franciscan Institute. Used by permission of the publisher. Excerpts from *Saint Bonaventure's Disputed Questions on the Mystery of the Trinity (Works of Saint Bonaventure)*, George Marcil, ed. Published by the Franciscan Institute. Used by permission of the publisher. Excerpts from "Incarnation and Creation in St. Bonaventure," in *Studies Honoring Ignatius Brady, Friar Minor*, Romano Stephen Almagno and Conrad L. Harkins, eds. Published by the Franciscan Institute. Used by permission of the publisher. Excerpts from *New Seeds of Contemplation*, copyright ©1961 by the Abbey of Gethsemani, Inc. Reprinted by permission of New Directions Publishing Corp. Excerpts from *Francis of Assisi: Early Documents*, volumes 1, 2 and 3 edited by Regis J. Armstrong, J.A. Wayne Hellmann and William J. Short, copyright ©1999. Reprinted with permission of New City Press. Excerpts from *The Grand Option: Personal Transformation and a New Creation* by Beatrice Bruteau. Copyright 2001 by University of Notre Dame, Notre Dame, IN 46556. Reprinted by permission. Excerpts from *Bonaventure: The Soul's Journey into God, The Tree of Life, The Life of St. Francis*, translation and introduction by Ewert Cousins; preface by Ignatius Brady, from the Classics of Western Spirituality, copyright ©1978 by Paulist Press, Inc., New York/Mahwah, N.J. Used with permission of Paulist Press. www.paulistpress.com.
Excerpts from "One of Us" by Eric Bazilian ©1995 by Human Boy Music (ASCAP). All rights on behalf of Human Boy Music (ASCAP). Administered by Alfred Publishing Co., Inc. All rights reserved. Used by permission.

Cover illustration by Darina Gladisová
Cover and book design by Mark Sullivan

Library of Congress Cataloging-in-Publication Data

Delio, Ilia.
    The humility of God : a Franciscan perspective / Ilia Delio.
        p. cm.
    Includes bibliographical references and index.
    ISBN 0-86716-675-4 (pbk. : alk. paper)
    1. Humility—Religious aspects—Christianity. 2. God. 3. Bonaventure, Saint, Cardinal, ca. 1217-1274. 4. Spirituality—Catholic Church. I. Title.

BV4647.H8D45 2005
231—dc22

                            2005010887

ISBN 978-0–86716–675–0

Published by Franciscan Media
28 W. Liberty St.
Cincinnati, OH 45202
www.FranciscanMedia.org

Contents

Acknowledgments

The idea of exploring the humility of God came to explicit consciousness in the summer of 2003 when Sister Kathleen Moffatt, O.S.F.
invited me to be part of a "Bonaventure Fest" sponsored by the Sisters
of St. Francis of Philadelphia and held at Neumann College. I am
grateful to Kathleen for organizing this tremendous event and to the
Sisters of St. Francis of Philadelphia for their generous support of the
conference. Their enthusiasm for the Franciscan intellectual tradition
continues to be infectious and is a great source of encouragement
for the pursuit of scholarship today. I am also deeply grateful to Dr.
Rosalie Mirenda, President of Neumann College, as well as the college
staff who graciously invited me to be part of their community during
my sabbatical time and provided a quiet and friendly environment to
write this book. I am especially thankful to Sisters Lynn Patrice Lavin,
O.S.F., Christopher Marie Wagner, O.S.F., Elaine Martin, O.S.F., and all
those who supported my work during my sabbatical. I am indebted to
Stephen Kluge, O.F.M., who read the initial text and raised questions
that enabled me to consider the content more carefully. I would like
to thank Zachary Hayes, O.F.M., for writing the preface to this book.
As one of the great Bonaventure scholars of our time, Father Hayes'
support of my work has been most humbly appreciated.

As I finished the first draft of this book my mother, Anne J. Delio,
slipped into a terminal state of congestive heart failure and gradually
released her grip on earthly life. Her death on the Vigil of Easter was
a shattering testimony to the power of the risen Christ. As I reflect on
her life I am reminded that the humility of God is the power of God's
unconditional love and that death is the unconditional surrender to that
love. My mother struggled with the humility of God in her lifetime, but
in her death she surrendered into the arms of love.

Preface

One of the crucial insights into the work of Saint Bonaventure that has emerged with the contemporary revival of interest in his work is the remarkable relation between his vision of spirituality and the highly intellectual dimensions of his work as a philosopher and a systematic theologian. This is one of the dimensions of the present treatment by Sister Ilia Delio that stands out in a remarkable way.

In looking at the title of this book, one might be reminded of a statement made by the philosopher Alfred N. Whitehead who spoke of the "brief Galilean vision of humility [that] flickered throughout the ages, uncertainly."[1] He contrasts this with the view that eventually won in Christianity, whereby, unfortunately, God was given the attributes that more properly belong to Caesar.[2] And more recently, Cardinal Ratzinger, in his reflections on the cross of Christ, is drawn to the implications of this mystery of the cross for our understanding of the divine. He does not hesitate to say that we will never fully understand the mystery with which we are confronted. But the mystery tells us something important about God. It tells us that "God does not simply rule by power.... His power is that of sharing in love and suffering.... God becomes small so that we can grasp his nature."[3]

Against this background, the work of Sister Ilia can be seen in terms of its deep spiritual and theological significance. One of her earlier books was entitled *Crucified Love: Bonaventure's Mysticism of the Crucified Christ*. Already here she points to the central significance of crucified love in the understanding of God. In the present book, she develops her thought more fully. Here the relation of Christ to the whole of the cosmos and its history becomes an important dimension of her presentation. She presents a genuinely cosmic Christology as she relates Christ to the whole of the cosmos and its history as viewed in the light of contemporary science. It is a world of evolution, of diversity, and a world marked by suffering.

From another perspective, crucial to her Christology is the internal relation of the mystery of the Incarnation to that of the divine Trinity. In this regard, she takes important insights from the Franciscan tradition, particularly from the work of Bonaventure as well as from the spiritual experience of Francis of Assisi. Though this is not an exclusively Franciscan treatise, it builds its rich reflections on many elements of that tradition, including Francis himself, together with the characteristic themes of the great theologians of the Order from medieval times. In Francis, Sister Ilia sees deep insight into the humility of God. This revolved around the encounter with Christ on the cross. She herself describes the present book as an attempt to "explore the humility of God...by way of Franciscan theology." In another formulation she says: "The humility of God is really about God's relationship to the world and God's fidelity to the world even when everything in the world seems to fail."

Here as in her previous work, Sister Ilia builds on her outstanding command of the scholarship about the work of Bonaventure, which has developed so remarkably in the twentieth century. Together with this she brings her personal knowledge and experience of contemporary scientific understandings of the cosmos. In a style that is preeminently readable, she offers insights into issues and problems that are widespread in the present period of Christian history. How, if at all, can well-educated Christians of the present era see the central symbols of their faith in relation to the worldview mediated to them by the best of the contemporary sciences? How, if at all, can a Christian believer relate faith in a God of creative love to a world so laden with pain and suffering? Sister Ilia has taken on these monumental issues and has opened insights that can be helpful to many who take their Christian faith seriously. For this, readers of this book about the humility of God will be deeply indebted to Sister Ilia.

—Zachary Hayes, O.F.M.

NOTES

[1] Alfred N. Whitehead, *Process and Reality* (The Free Press: New York, 1969), p. 404.

[2] Alfred N. Whitehead, *Adventures of Ideas* (The Free Press: New York, 1967), pp. 166–167.

[3] Joseph Cardinal Ratzinger (Pope Benedict XVI), Peter Seewald, Henry Tyler (trans.), *God and the World: Believing and Living in our Time* (Ignatius Press. San Francisco, 2002), pp. 338–339.

Introduction

Children have a way sometimes of asking questions that get right to the heart of things. Recently I heard the story of a little boy who, intrigued by the idea of God, went to his mother and asked, "What is God's last name?" The mother was perplexed and unable to answer her small son's difficult question. Then he said to her, "I know what it is. God's last name is 'World'!" I am sure this little boy had no idea that his answer was profound but the fact is theologians and philosophers today are still scratching their heads trying to come up with God's "last name." A last name signifies the identity of a person. The singer Joan Osborne sang, "If God had a name what would it be and would you call it to his face if you were faced with him in all his glory, what would you ask if you had just one question?" (words and music by Eric M. Bazilian).[1] Would you name God as "God-World"? And would you ask him, "why is your last name 'World'"? These questions in a sense form the background to this book on the humility of God. Although it is not an attempt to name God, it is an effort to understand why God's last name is "World" and how this last name contributes to the "identity" of God as humble love. The humility of God is really about God's relationship to the world and God's fidelity to the world, even when everything in the world seems to fail.

There are probably many ways to discuss the humility of God; however, when we look at it through the lens of Franciscan theology we see that the humility of God tells us something not only of God but our lives as well. The Franciscan view of God's humility combines a theology and spirituality of humility that is centered in Christ because

Christ is *God-with-us*. It is for this reason, I believe, that it provides not only a hopeful way of living in relation to God in a world of change but also a way of living a meaningful Christian life in a complex and often fragmented world.

Although this is not the first book on the humility of God, it is the first book that explores the theology of God's humility from a Franciscan perspective. I have chosen the particular lens of Bonaventure's theology for several reasons. First, it is Bonaventure's theology I know best so it is appropriate to speak out of an area of familiarity. Second, Bonaventure's Christ-centered mysticism is relevant to the search for God today in a fast-paced, scientific world that, in many ways, views God as an unnecessary hypothesis. Every theology is a lens of interpretation, a way to view the deep connections between God and world. Bonaventure's theology is a rich synthesis of God, humanity and creation with Christ as center. Because his synthesis is "Christ-centered" it impels us to recognize the significance of the humanity of Christ for understanding the God-world relationship.

For those who are unfamiliar with Bonaventure a brief introduction is worthwhile.[2]

Bonaventure of Bagnoregio was a Franciscan scholar and theologian of the thirteenth century. He was a follower of Francis of Assisi, the popular saint of the Middle Ages who attracted a myriad of followers and legends to go with him. Bonaventure was impressed by the poverty and humility of Francis' life and sought to follow his way of life. He was educated in theology at the University of Paris where he studied under some of the leading masters of his age, including the renowned Alexander of Hales. As a scholastic theologian, Bonaventure wrote commentaries on the *Sentences* of Peter Lombard (a "must" for all theology students at that time) and engaged in disputed questions (dialectical arguments) on various theological questions. He composed sermons for various feasts and wrote a number of spiritual works, including the *Major Legend of Saint Francis* and the classic *Soul's Journey into God*.

The most prominent theme of Bonaventure's theology is the centrality of Christ crucified and he devoted a number of spiritual writings to developing this theme. Bonaventure's understanding of Christ was closer to the Eastern Fathers of the church than to the theologians of the west. He viewed Christ less as a remedy for sin and more as the goal and center of the universe. Christ came, he said, to complete the universe as well as to save us from sin. Christ is the Word of God, the Alpha and Omega, the One through whom all things are made and in whom all things return to God. "Christ is not ordained to us," Bonaventure wrote, rather "we are ordained to Christ."[3] The purpose of the universe is bound to the mystery of Christ.

This notion of Christ as the head of creation took on more explicit formulation in the work of another Franciscan, Duns Scotus, a thirteenth-century philosopher. It was Scotus who brought to attention the "primacy of Christ," a doctrine rooted in the writings of Saint Paul (Ephesians 1:3–14; Colossians 1:15–20) and some of the early church Fathers (Irenaeus of Lyons, Origen of Alexandria, and Maximus the Confessor). The doctrine of the primacy of Christ means that Jesus did not come because of human sin; rather, from all eternity God willed to love a finite other as a more perfect expression of his love. Jesus would have come, therefore, even if there had been no sin. The meaning of the Incarnation is not about sin but about the love of God.

The idea that Christ is first in God's intention to love gives a positive spin to the God-world relationship. The Franciscan theologian Zachary Hayes writes:

> God creates so that Christ may come into existence. So
> that Christ may exist, there must be a human race. But a
> human race needs a place in which to live. So it is that, for
> both Bonaventure and Scotus, though for each in a distinc-
> tive way, a cosmos without Christ is a cosmos without its
> head.... It simply does not hold together.[4]

All of creation is made for Christ. The whole universe is oriented toward Christ. The Jesuit scientist and mystic Pierre Teilhard de Chardin described a Christ-centered universe as an evolutionary universe moving toward the fullness of Christ. Teilhard spoke of Christ as the Omega Point—Christ is not only the plan for creation but the goal of creation.[5] Love is the energizing force in the universe and the fullness of Christ is the goal toward which the universe tends. It is because of the Incarnation, he claimed, that "nothing here below is profane for those who know how to see."[6] Although Teilhard was not a Franciscan, his notion of a Christic universe[7] complements Bonaventure's theology of the Incarnation in light of the humility of God. I therefore look to Teilhard to draw out the contemporary implications of Franciscan theology for our world today.

It is in light of Christ as the meaning and goal of the universe that the humility of God finds its significance; the humility of God is intertwined with the Incarnation. Bonaventure describes the humility of God through the words of John's Gospel "the Word was made flesh" (John 1:14). He writes:

> These words give expression to that heavenly mystery and that admirable sacrament, that magnificent work of infinite kindness, which consists in the fact that *the eternal God has humbly bent down* and lifted the dust of our nature into unity with His own person. The term "Word" designates the person who assumes, while "flesh" designates what it was that He assumed, and "made" points to the actual assumption or union.[8]

In the Incarnation, Bonaventure says, God bends down to embrace us in love. We might say that God's last name is "World" because when the Word becomes flesh, the Word through whom all things are created becomes visibly expressed in created reality. When the Word enters into created reality—the world—God's identity is revealed. We come to know that God is love or, we might say, God is humble love. To understand the meaning of God's humble love in the world is the purpose of this book. Let us take a brief look at the chapters to see what awaits us.

Because this is a book rooted in Franciscan theology, the first chapter examines God's humility through the theological intuitions of Francis of Assisi. Francis was certainly not a trained theologian but he was, what we call today, a "vernacular theologian."[9] He had profound experiences of God and he articulated those experiences in his own words. One of the main experiences of God that Francis spoke about in his writings is God's "humility." Francis discovered the humility of God through his encounter with Jesus Christ, especially the Christ on the cross. He described the mystery of the triune God as sublime and humble, ineffable and immanent, a mystery of opposites, which he grasped through his insight to Christ as Son, Word and wisdom of the Father. The most profound expression of God's humility for Francis was in the Eucharist and he described this mystery of God's humble presence, this "Body of Christ," as the principal sacrament of God and the means of relationship to God.

Francis' insight to the humility of God was influential on Bonaventure. Eric Doyle once described the relationship between Francis and Bonaventure as "the disciple and the Master," a description that captures the spiritual bond between these two mystic-saints. Bonaventure took the theme of divine humility and developed it in light of the Trinity of love. He continuously explored love as the reason for both creation and the Incarnation. The Incarnation, according to Bonaventure, is not the movement of love in a general sense but in the particular form of humility. The humility of God expresses itself not only in the event of the Incarnation but in its concrete form, the humility and poverty of Christ. The humility of Christ leads us into the humility of God.

In the second chapter I examine the humble heart of God as the heart of the Trinity. To appreciate the humility of God it is helpful to understand Bonaventure's Trinitarian theology, especially in view of relationships of love. A deeper insight into these relationships shows us that humility is not a quality of God, it is an essential aspect of God's nature as love. It is out of the love relationship between the Father and Son that creation emerges. Just as the Word expresses the Father, creation finitely expresses the infinite Word of God. The complementary relationship Bonaventure describes between the divine Word and creation involves the mystery of God's humble relationship to the world. When the Word becomes flesh, God bends over in love to lift up not only human nature but creation itself which the human body extends. All of created reality expresses in some way the humility of God because all of created reality expresses in some way the Word of God.

The relationship between the Trinity of humble love and creation is a relationship of opposites (fullness and emptiness) that finds union in the person of Jesus Christ. Chapter three looks at the Incarnation from the point of God's humble love revealed in Christ and Christ as the meaning of the cosmos. Bonaventure's metaphor of Christ as the "Book of Life" is helpful to discuss the significance of Christ for us, especially as the meaning of Christ unfolds in the life of Francis. By focusing on the meaning of Christ in terms of love and completion of the universe, I then look more closely at Bonaventure's idea that the fullness of Christ includes the entirety of humanity and creation. Bonaventure used a technical term *convenientia* to describe the congruent or "made-to-fit" relationship between the Word of God and the human person in whom the Word comes to dwell in an explicit way. In several of his sermons and spiritual writings he explores this congruent relationship in such a way that we are led to conclude that the mystery of Christ is not an isolated, autonomous, self-sufficient mystery. As the mystery of divinity and humanity united in a single Person, the mystery of Christ includes all those united in Christ and in a more broadly conceived way, the whole creation. To state this simply, the fullness of the mystery of Christ is completed in humanity; thus, it depends on us human beings and our participation in the mystery of Christ. Because the non-human material world depends on us humans for its completion in God, it, too, is part of the mystery of Christ but can only participate in this mystery in and through the human person. How does this relationship between Christ and humanity relate to the humility of God? Well, if God bends over in love for us in and through the Word incarnate, then we who are little "words" must bend over in love for one another and for all creation if the universe is to find its fulfillment in Christ. God's humble love must live in us through grace and freedom.

Having laid out the theology of the humility of God in the first three chapters, I then proceed to discuss the significance of God's humility in a world of evolution, suffering and plurality. In a sense these next three chapters underlie the core of this book, which is not only to explore the humility of God, but to explore the humility of God in a fragmented, complex and changing world. There are many

"God questions" around but I have chosen to focus on the questions that seem most urgent. The first question concerns the place of God in an evolutionary universe. The new science today tells us that the universe is ancient and expanding. It began billions of years ago and will likely continue for billions of years into the future. Biological evolution tells us that nature has built-in means of regulating its growth, such as natural selection, chance and mutation. Many systems are self-regulating with inherent feedback mechanisms that signal when to turn on, when to turn off and when to shut down. In the area of quantum mechanics we know that chance and uncertainty are part of the physical fabric of the universe. Chaos theory tells us that disorder is a welcome change in open systems. Disorder can be the stimulus for new order that appears slowly over time due to basins of attraction that lie within open systems. Throughout these various levels of disorder, chance and uncertainty questions are raised. What is God doing? Does God design or control all the intricate systems of creation or does God simply allow creation to be? Is there a role for God in creation? These are some of the major questions being discussed in the area of religion and science today. For our purposes, however, we will entertain these questions more broadly in view of the humility of God and discuss how God might "act" in a world of evolution and complexity.

The second area of concern is the role of God in a suffering world. The book of Job reminds us that good people are vulnerable to suffering. The September 11 terrorist attacks tell us that our lives are contingent and finite; we may go to work one morning and never return. While we live in an age of terrorism, we have emerged from one of the bloodiest centuries of history. The twentieth century, marked by two world wars, still bears the scars of the viciousness of humanity, from the concentration camps at Auschwitz and Dachau to the killing fields of Cambodia. The human person has the capacity for greatness but also the capacity for brutal violence. While war and terrorism form one level of suffering, there are many other levels. The widespread epidemic of AIDS in Africa and Asia today is annihilating whole generations of men and women; the high rate of cancer due to the proliferation of chemicals in our environment and foods, among other factors, is alarming.

There are stress-related illnesses, mental illness, Alzheimer's disease, physical disabilities, the difficulties of old age, and the list can go on. In all these areas people suffer. The question is, where is God in all of this human suffering? Is God indifferent to human suffering? How about the suffering of the earth, the pillaging and stripping of natural resources? Is this of concern to God? Like the challenges of the new science today, the questions of suffering are broad and not easily addressed. However, looking at the question of suffering from the view of God's humble love may give us a better insight as to how God relates to a world of suffering. Bonaventure's profound emphasis on the crucified Christ indicates to us that God is no stranger to suffering and, indeed, the cross is the hope of new life in God. In chapter five, therefore, we will explore God's involvement in a world of suffering through the lens of Bonaventure and Francis. We will discuss God's compassionate love in the world and the way this love finds its root in the heart of the Trinity.

The sixth chapter takes up the role of God's humility in a world of pluralism and difference. We have entered into a "global age" and it is unlikely that we will turn back at any point in the future. Today we hear the terms "global spirituality," "global economy," "globalization" and, although we may not be entirely sure of what these various terms mean, we know that our little corner of American soil is no longer a white, western European, Protestant territory but rather encompasses Asians, Africans, Hispanics and peoples from around the world. The products we buy are made in such places as China, the Philippines and Mexico, often coming from poor areas of the world where laborers are grossly underpaid for products that are sold at exorbitant prices.

I live in the area of Washington, D.C., which is a kaleidoscope of various cultures, languages and ethnicities. Is everyone Catholic? No. Is everyone Christian? No. So what does a humble God of love do in such a diverse world? Rejoice! Because God's creation is a wonderful celebration of diversity. Our God is not a boring God! But somehow our Catholic doctrine still creates walls of separation, paths of exclusivity, "in" and "out" groups. By exploring the relationship of a humble God to a world of difference we come to a more broadly conceived notion of the meaning of Christ.

In this chapter we examine the meaning of Christ in light of plurality and difference through the life of Francis of Assisi. While Francis did not live in an age of globalism, he did live in a society of class distinctions. Through his life in Christ he came to see that Christ cannot be limited to a single human person; rather, Christ encompasses the whole creation. Nowhere is this more evident than in his *Canticle of the Creatures*. By entering into the heart of Christ, Francis found Christ at the heart of the world. The life of Francis indicates to us that to be a Christian is to find Christ in every person and living creature, and to be in union with Christ is to experience God's goodness throughout creation, not just in a church. Christ, the risen incarnate Word of God, encompasses the whole creation and until we live in relation to *this* Christ we will continue to experience the increasing irrelevance of Christianity.

The importance of living in relation to Christ, the Living One, at the center of the universe is discussed in the final two chapters. In chapter seven I attempt to interpret the Christian vocation today in light of the humility of God in an evolutionary universe. I entitled this chapter "Christic Christians" because a Christian [noun] is not necessarily engaged in Christian life. The "Christic" [adjective] Christian, however, is one who lives out of a God-center, one in whom Christ lives anew, and this person is actively engaged in "christifying" the universe, helping it achieve its goal in Christ so that God may be all in all.[10] Again, aspects of the life of Francis are helpful to bring us to deeper insight of a broadly conceived notion of Christian life, especially as Bonaventure described Francis searching for God and finding him hidden in all the broken places of humanity. What we see through the lens of Francis is that Christian life requires active engagement; to be attentive to the humility of God who hides in ordinary fragile human flesh, tiny creatures and the natural elements of creation.

Drawing upon the insights of Teilhard de Chardin and Ewert Cousins, I discuss the significance of the humility of God in light of global consciousness and a universe that is Christ-centered. As Teilhard never tired of reminding us, Christ is not an unrelated intrusion into the universe but the continuation and fulfillment of a long cosmic preparation. The universe is in evolution toward the fullness of

Christ but it is the task of Christians to help personalize the universe in the love of Christ. Christianity, we might say, is a religion of evolution and a religion of the future. The good news of Jesus Christ is that suffering and death do not have the last word. The last word is life and the fullness of life in God. The question is: How do we attain the fullness of life in God? Is it in the future, and only if we are good? Is it reserved for heaven-bound travelers? Is it only for Christians, those who profess belief in Christ? In this chapter, therefore, we explore the meaning of Christian life in a new age of consciousness and the role of the Christian in an evolutionary universe.

The final chapter continues the theme of the Christian vocation in light of the humility of God but with a specific view toward divinization. The concept of divinization was quite popular among the early writers of the church who held that God became human so that humans could become divine. However, divinization seems to have dropped out of sight. It is seldom discussed and even more seldom aspired to. I rarely hear of anyone who wants to be *divinized* or who sets out to achieve this goal. Yet, divinization is what Christian life is ultimately about. The universe continues to falter and stumble in its movement toward Christ because we Christians are unaware that to be divinized is to live passionately, to be intimately involved in the world, to sacrifice our lives if necessary for the sake of the gospel. Divinization contradicts any culture that thrives on privatism and individualism. ("What? You want me to sacrifice my life for something other than my own immediate pleasure? Are you kidding?") Chapter eight, therefore, examines the goal of divinization by first discussing what it means to be an image of God. Bonaventure develops the notion of the image of God in a way that is closer to the Eastern theologian Gregory of Nyssa than to Augustine, whose theology of image predominates in the west.

The basis of image for Bonaventure is Christ and, like Gregory, he sees that Christ is the one image in whom every person finds his or her true image in God. To be divinized, we might say, is to be in union with Christ in love, to imitate Christ, so that, ultimately, there is one image, one Christ, to the glory of the Father. Again, insights from the life of Francis help us appreciate the meaning of being an image and likeness of God, which Bonaventure develops in terms of love and conformity to Christ. By reflecting on the meaning of divinization for Christian life in an evolutionary universe, we see that to live in God's humble love is to live in attentiveness, openness and relationship: attentiveness to the presence of God in the details of the fragile human person, openness to the ways God is both hidden and revealed in creation, and relationship to the God incarnated in our neighbors, family and community members. In each of these areas we are called to love in a spirit of compassion, forgiveness, tenderness and care. As God bends low to love us where we are, we must be open to welcome God in our lives, to embrace this God of humble love and to allow God to live in us in every way. Every breath of life must be the breath of God. This is divinization. The humility of God's love in some way demands a human response because it is hidden and unobtrusive and quietly sustains life without force or manipulation. It is the role of Christians to publicly witness to the humility of God's faithful love, and this is nothing short of making Christ live anew. As Gregory of Nyssa wrote, "Christianity is the imitation of God's nature."[11]

In his spiritual work *The Tree of Life* Bonaventure said that humility is the root and guardian of all virtues.[12] By this statement he meant that Christian life must be grounded in humility if God is to be the center of the life. By "humility" Bonaventure meant a self-knowledge grounded in truth, patience with others, simplicity of life, attentive listening to others, courage to overcome temptations and a compassionate heart.[13] Jesus, he claimed, is the teacher of humility.[14] In Bonaventure's view, only the poor and humble can share in the humble love of God. Yet, humility is not a virtue we strive for, it is not a popular fad in our culture. It can be easily labeled "pious dribble" and placed on dusty ledges together with outmoded devotional prayer books. Humility, in popular terms, is not "cool."

It is my hope, however, that a Franciscan view of humility—God's humble love and our response to that love—can lead to new insight with regard to God's presence in our world and our Christian vocation. Francis of Assisi wanted to be a "brother minor" so that he could humbly bend down in solidarity with all living creatures of the earth. We, too, are called to bend low in love, to find the humble love of God in the simple ordinary and oftentimes broken hearts of the world. To do so, however, we must be free to bend low in love. In Christ, God has set us free. It is up to us as Christians to live in the freedom of God's humble love. Only by living in the freedom of love can we help transform the world into the fullness of Christ. It is possible. Francis did it in his own way and in his own time. Now we, too, must do the same.

NOTES

[1] Joan Osborne, *Relish.* "If God Was One of Us," written by Eric M. Bazilian. (New York: Mercury/Universal, 1995).

[2] A longer introduction can be found in my book *Simply Bonaventure: An Introduction to His Life, Thought and Writings* (New York: New City Press, 2001), pp. 21–35.

[3] Bonaventure, III *Sentences (Sent.)* d. 32, q. 5, ad 3 (III, 706). "*Humanum vero genus respectu incarnationis et nativitatis Christi non fuit ratio finaliter movens, sed quodam modo inducens. Non enim Christus ad nos finaliter, sed nos finaliter ordinamur ad ipsum.*" The critical edition of Bonaventure's works is the *Opera Omnia* ed. PP. Collegii S. Bonaventurae, 10 vols. (Quaracchi, 1882–1902). Latin texts are indicated by volume and page number in parentheses.

[4] Zachary Hayes, "Christ, Word of God and Exemplar of Humanity: The Roots of Franciscan Christocentrism and its Implications for Today," *The Cord* 46.1 (1996): 13.

[5] Pierre Teilhard de Chardin, "My Universe," in *Process Theology: Basic Writings*, Ewert H. Cousins, ed. (New York: Newman Press, 1971), pp. 249–55; Donald P. Gray, *The One and the Many: Teilhard de Chardin's Vision of Unity* (New York: Herder and Herder, 1969), pp. 95–107.

[6] Pierre Teilhard de Chardin, *The Divine Milieu*, Bernard Wall, trans. (New York: Harper and Row, 1960), p. 66.

[7] Henri de Lubac, *Teilhard de Chardin: The Man and His Meaning*, René Hague, trans. (New York: Hawthorn Books, 1966), p. 29. Teilhard used the term *Christic* to describe the personal presence of God in the universe.

[8] Bonaventure, "Sermon II on the Nativity of the Lord," in *What Manner of Man? Sermons on Christ by St. Bonaventure*, Zachary Hayes, trans. (Chicago: Franciscan Herald Press, 1989), p. 57. Emphasis added.

[9] For a description of Francis as vernacular theologian see Dominic V. Monti, "Francis as Vernacular Theologian: A Link to the Franciscan Intellectual Tradition," in *The Franciscan Intellectual Tradition*, Elise Saggau, ed. (New York: The Franciscan Institute, 2001), pp. 21–42.

[10] William Thompson describes the Christic self as a self wholly integrated into God and into the world in which we live. For a discussion on the Christic self, see William M. Thompson, *Jesus as Lord and Savior: A Theopathic Christology and Soteriology* (New York: Paulist, 1980), pp. 162–192.

[11] Gregory of Nyssa, *De Professione Christiana*, cited in Vladimir Lossky, *Orthodox Theology:*

An Introduction, Ian and Ihita Kesarcodi-Watson, trans. (Crestwood, N.Y.: St. Vladimir's Seminary Press, 1978), p. 128.

[12] Bonaventure *Lignum vitae (Lig. vit.)* 5 (VIII, 72). Ewert Cousins, trans. *Bonaventure: The Soul's Journey into God, The Tree of Life, The Major Life of St. Francis* (New York: Paulist, 1978), p. 129 hereafter referred to as *Lig. vit.*

[13] Bonaventure *Lig. vit.* 8–10 (VIII, 72–73).

[14] Bonaventure *Lig. vit.* 7 (VIII, 72).

Chapter One

A HIDDEN GOD

If God had a name, what would it be
And would you call it to his face
If you were faced with him in all his glory
What would you ask if you had just one question
—Sung by Joan Osborne, written by Eric M. Bazilian,
 "One of Us"

Did you ever have one of those days where the whole idea of God was just too much to think about? As if trying to "get a handle" on God was like trying to kiss the moon? If the mystics are right (and usually they are because they see things much differently than we do) then you were probably closer that day to God than any other day in your life. How is this possible, you ask? How can God be close to you (or you to God) when God seems so far away or not at all? Even better, how can God be close to you when you are totally confused? This is my answer to you: God is a mystery of humble love. It is a mystery that you cannot reason or try to figure out. You must simply live in the mystery. This is my hope for you and my reason for writing to you—that you may live in the mystery of God's humble love.

First, I need to ask you this: What is your image of God at the present moment? How do you picture God? Is God something like your Father only older and wiser? Does God have white hair and a goatee? Or is God more like your mother? A gentle, caring God but one who is always after you about what you are wearing, what you are doing or where you going? I myself am often startled by the images we have of God. The prophet Isaiah, for example, writes, "Here is the Lord Yahweh coming with power, his arm subduing all things to him" (Isaiah 40:10). It is quite intimidating to think that God rules by a "strong arm." One swift swing of the arm and we can be turned into dust. But then Isaiah also describes God as a gentle, caring God:

> I have called you by name, you are mine.
> Should you pass through the sea, I will be with you;
> or through rivers, they will not swallow you up.
> Should you walk through fire, you will be scorched and
> the flames will not burn you.
> For I am Yahweh, your God,
> the Holy One of Israel, your savior. (Isaiah 43:2–3)

These words are indeed a sign of God's comforting presence.

The problem with God is that sometimes we think we know who God is and other times we are totally baffled by the mere thought of God. I believe that many people relate to God according to the time of day, month of year, or stage of life. At some stages of life, God is thought of as good, lovable, kind, gentle and merciful, a protector and friend who is close at hand. And yet at other stages, God may be thought of as harsh, unfair, aloof, merciless and really not necessary in a world that has so many problems. We often make God in our own image and this makes God a projection of ourselves. Freud wasn't wrong after all.

But the mystics tell us otherwise. The sixth-century mystic Pseudo-Dionysius (whose identity we still don't know) said that as soon as we say something about God like "God is my rock" or "God is light," we must put these thoughts aside for God is much greater than a rock or much more than light.[1] God, Pseudo-Dionysius said, is incomprehensible, beyond our language and imagination, beyond anything we can describe. The only language appropriate to address God is silence. We who think silence means absence of speech are, according to Pseudo-Dionysius, improperly informed. Only in silence can we enter into the great mystery we call "God." The great vast realms of silence where God dwells means that God is much more than a bigger version of

Moses or Abraham. God is beyond Being, beyond our imagination, beyond the limits of our speech. If you want to talk to God, Pseudo-Dionysius said, don't say anything at all. God will listen. Too often our prayers are projections of our own needs and desires and we give God little room to enter into the conversation. Talking all the time to God without ever listening is like a phone conversation with constant static; it is deafening to God. Silence is a language God can speak without being constantly interrupted because God is a mystery of incomprehensible love, and love speaks for itself. If we could really be attentive to the mystery of God in our lives we would realize that God is both beyond our thoughts and imaginations (although these can bring us closer to God) and very near to us. As Saint Augustine indicated, God is closer to us than we are to ourselves.[2] God is a mystery of silence and intimacy. God is incomprehensible and ineffable, far beyond our wildest imaginations, yet nearer to each of us than we are to ourselves.

I think Francis of Assisi grasped something of the mystery of God and, in a particular way, the mystery of God's humility. Although he was simple and not well educated, he had an insight into God that I can only say was profound. Francis did not study theology. He did not try to figure out what God is through reason. He simply spent long hours in prayer, often in caves, mountains or places of solitude, places where he could distance himself from the busy everyday world. Thomas of Celano, the first biographer of Francis, wrote: "Where the knowledge of teachers is outside, the passion of the lover entered."[3] What Thomas perceived is that love, not knowledge, allowed Francis to enter into the great mystery we call "God." As he entered into this mystery he discovered two principle features of God—the overflowing goodness of God and the humility of God. That is why a Franciscan approach to God's humility must begin with Francis. For he was so impressed by God's humility that he spent his entire life striving to live humbly in imitation of God. How did a man as simple as Francis arrive at this mystery of God? The answer is Jesus Christ. Francis came to know the God of humble love by meditating on and imitating the poor and humble Christ. It is helpful to know something of Francis' story in order to appreciate his deep insight into God.

Francis' life story has been told so often throughout the centuries and in so many different versions that someone once asked, "did Francis of Assisi really exist?"[4] The biographical accounts composed for the Franciscan Order, however, remain most reliable. Thomas of Celano, a friar who wrote shortly after Francis' death, composed the first life of Francis and Bonaventure of Bagnoregio, after becoming Minister General, wrote the official biography for the Franciscan Order.[5] According to Celano, Francis was not a particularly religious young man. Instead, he liked fun parties, "practical jokes and foolish talk, songs, and soft and flowing garments."[6] He was a dreamer and a seeker of fortune. Celano says that "he vowed, out of vainglory and vanity, to do great deeds."[7] Apparently, he wanted to become a valiant knight but was wounded in battle. He spent a year in convalescence and it was during this time that he began to reflect on his life, its meaning and purpose. Something happened deep within him during this time that changed him. Bonaventure says that he had a dream in which Christ appeared to him and asked him why he was following the servant (the leader of the army) instead of the master (Christ himself). Whatever it was that changed within Francis, the best we can say is that the grace of God touched his heart and he began to take up a life of penance or conversion. He moved out of his father's house, renounced his paternity and initially took up the life of a wandering hermit. He began to enter abandoned churches and spent long hours in prayer. Eventually he felt called to preach the gospel and became a poor, itinerant preacher with a small band of followers.

One day he entered the brokendown church of San Damiano on the outskirts of his hometown, Assisi. There, in the center of the church, was a large Byzantine cross with the figure of Christ crucified and glorified. He heard the image of Christ crucified speak to him. "'Francis,' it said, calling him by name, 'go rebuild My house; as you can see, it is all being destroyed.' Francis was stunned by these words. He felt a mysterious change in himself," Celano writes, "but he could not describe it."[8] Bonaventure says that one day while Francis was praying in a solitary place, Christ Jesus appeared to him fastened to a cross. "His *soul melted* at the sight, and the memory of Christ's passion was so impressed on the innermost recesses of his heart. From that hour, whenever Christ's crucifixion came to his mind, he could scarcely contain his tears and sighs."[9] Celano, too, said that after the encounter with Christ crucified in the church of San Damiano, Francis wept loudly over the passion of Christ, "as if it were constantly before his eyes."[10] Who really knows what happened to Francis in that church or when he was alone at prayer? All we can say is that God bent low to kiss Francis when he least expected it. An unexpected kiss can change one's life forever.

Francis lived in the spirit of humility and poverty by following the poor and humble Christ. In his *Major Legend of Saint Francis,* Bonaventure says that after Francis was impressed with the passion of Christ "he… showed deeds of humility and humanity to lepers with a gentle piety… with a great drive of compassion [he] kissed their hands and their mouths."[11] Bonaventure uses the symbol of the kiss to indicate that Francis discovered the sweetness of God hidden in the bitter flesh of the leper. Just as God reached out to embrace Francis in the compassionate love of the cross, so, too, that same God was now present in the distorted figure of the leper. Touched by grace, Francis became open to the otherness of the leper as the experience of self-transcendence, that is, as the experience of God. The leper became a source of God's loving embrace and thus someone to whom Francis realized he was intimately related. He therefore began to identify with the leper as brother. At the end of his life, Francis confessed that after showing mercy to the lepers, "what had seemed bitter was turned into sweetness of soul and body."[12] We might say that the bitterness of the leper's flesh was made sweet when Francis recognized God's infinite goodness in it.

The leper experience was a turning point in Francis' life. As his life deepened in God, he made a constant effort to spend himself in love by giving himself to the other. He became bent over in love for every person, every creature, including tiny earthworms which he would pick up so that they would not be crushed underfoot.[13] By following the poor and humble Christ, Francis was formed into a "brother minor." His followers said that he became "another Christ" because, like Christ, he was humble in love. Following the footprints of Jesus, Francis found the God of humble love not among the popular and the proud, the arrogant and the rich or those who "stand out" in society but among the ordinary, the forgotten, the poor and sick and the marginalized. The God of Francis, Celano wrote, was a God "who delights to be / with *the simple* and those rejected by the world."[14] Although Francis made every effort to follow Christ, the footprints of Christ he followed were not shallow but deeply God-centered. To understand the humility of God for Francis, it is important to see how Francis grasped this mystery in his own words.

Throughout his writings, Francis indicates that God is the central reality from whom everything comes and toward whom everything converges.[15] Francis had many names for God: "merciful, gentle, delightful, sweet, just, true, holy, and upright, innocent, clean,"[16] but the one name that stood out was "good." Francis perceived that God is a mystery of inexhaustible goodness. In his "Earlier Rule" he spoke of God as the "fullness of good, / all good, every good, the true and supreme good."[17] God is overflowing goodness. The highest good of course is love. So really what Francis was saying is that "God is love," or better, "God is a mystery of love." Francis' journey was a life of striving to love God. He used to go about the world saying: "the love of him who loved us greatly is greatly to be loved!"[18] Love is a mystery. When you love someone you know him in a deeper way; yet, the more you know someone the less you truly know him. The more the face of the lover is revealed, the more it is concealed. And so it is with God. The more we come to know the God of love, the more we are confronted with the mystery of God as a mystery of opposites: knowable and unknowable, ineffable and describable, utterly transcendent and supremely good. Through the door of love Francis entered into the mystery of God, the mystery of unity and Trinity, the mystery of God as one and three. He described the Trinity as "awesome," "most high," "supreme," and "most holy," a mystery beyond human expression and comprehension. In his "Earlier Rule" he wrote:

> the Most High and Supreme Eternal God
> Trinity and Unity,

Father, Son and Holy Spirit,
without beginning and end,
is unchangeable, invisible
indescribable, ineffable,
incomprehensible, unfathomable.[19]

When we read these words, we are struck by Francis' understanding of God as incomprehensible, ineffable and transcendent. God is Trinity beyond our most creative imaginations, beyond the limits of our language, beyond any idea we can conceive. Yet, God is not beyond our human experience because God is personal—Father, Son and Spirit. God is, indeed, a mystery of opposites because God is a mystery of love.

Francis discovered the God of personal love through revelation. He truly believed that God was made known to us in Jesus Christ.[20] He came to know the Father as the Most High because of the Son, Jesus Christ and he had a personal relationship to the Father in a way that was both deeply reverential and intimate.[21] He understood revelation as the movement of the Father to us in the Son. Although he often spoke of God the Father, he never perceived the Father to be a lonely figure, detached from the Son. What Francis understood is that the Son, Jesus Christ, is always in relationship with the Father for this is what the Gospel says: "No one knows who the Son is except the Father, and who the Father is except the Son and those to whom the Son chooses to reveal him" (Luke 10:22). In order to come to any knowledge or relationship with the Father, therefore, Francis realized he would have to come to know the Son—even better—to become like the Son, that is, to become an "adopted" child of the Father.

For Francis, this relationship with the Father through the Son could not take place without the Spirit. He knew that where the Father and Son is, so, too, is the Spirit. It is the Spirit who enables us to follow in the Son's footsteps in order to return to the Most High Father. He wrote: "inflamed by the fire of the Holy Spirit / may we be able to follow / in the footprints of your beloved Son, / our Lord Jesus Christ, / and, by Your grace alone, / may we make our way to You, / Most

High."[22] The Spirit cleanses, enlightens and finally sets on fire the innermost recesses of our souls. It is the Spirit's grace and light that foster "the holy virtues" in our hearts, changing us from being "faithless" into being "faithful to God." And it is in the "charity of the Spirit" that we know God's love for us.[23] All of this is to say that when Francis addressed himself to God the Father, he did so in view of the Trinity. He emphasized the Father's love for the Son—the beloved Son—and realized that God loves us not apart from this Son but precisely in and through the Son.

Francis did not see himself far removed from God's love. Rather, he saw that the movement of the Father's love for the Son, the reaching out of the Father for the Son, is the same movement of love that reached out to Francis and continues to reach out and embrace us humans and creation.[24] The love of the Father for the Son is the same divine love for all creation. In his "Earlier Rule" he prayed:

All-powerful, most holy,
Almighty and supreme God,
Holy and just *Father*,
Lord King *of heaven and earth*
we thank You for Yourself
for through Your holy will
and through Your only Son
with the Holy Spirit
You have created everything spiritual and corporal

. . .

We thank You
for as through Your Son You created us,
so through Your holy love
with which You loved us
You brought about His birth
as true God and true man[25]

This is quite an incredible insight—to realize that we are embraced by the Father through the Son. Our lives, according to Francis, are enveloped in the mystery of the Son for it is the Son who pleases the

Father in everything. God is a God of prodigal love who longs for our return and reaches out with open arms, but the only way we can enter this embrace is through the Spirit who joins us to the Son who then leads us to the Father.

Whenever we speak about love, we are speaking about relationship. Bonaventure wrote that love is the gravity of the soul; it is what pulls us toward God.[26] We could also say that love is the glue of the universe; it is what constantly holds everything together even when things fall apart. It is simply impossible to think of love sitting on an island all alone. Love likes company. Love means going out to the other for the sake of the other. But there are different types of love. For example, there is love of the other for one's self, which is a type of desirous or erotic love, or there is love of the other for the sake of the other— *agapic*, or compassionate, love. God is both *eros* and *agape*.[27] God desires our love and yet is compassionate in love. Francis believed that God is love; therefore, God is Trinity. The love of the Father is revealed in the Son who always seeks to do the will of the Father (out of love) and sends the Spirit as witness to the truth of God as love in the hearts of believers. The persons of the Trinity are so united in love that everything they do—creation, redemption, salvation—they do together in love, out of love and for love. It is because the persons of the Trinity are so united in love that Francis understood the Incarnation, the Word made flesh, as the love of the Trinity expressed in a human person. The Trinity does not become "undone" in the Incarnation, as if the three divine persons split up and take on different jobs. What Francis understood is that the whole Trinity is revealed in the Incarnation. In a letter to his followers he wrote:

> The most high father made known from heaven through His holy angel, Gabriel, this Word of the Father—so worthy, so holy and glorious—in the womb of the holy and glorious Virgin Mary, from whose womb He received the flesh of our humanity and frailty. Though He was rich, He wished, together with the most Blessed Virgin, His mother, to choose poverty in the world beyond all else.[28]

What strikes one immediately in this passage is the intimate relationship between the Father and Son—the Father "announces" the Word made flesh. He could have said that the Father sent the Son to humanity to save us, but that would have a different meaning. That would make the Father more remote, as if the Father was a stage manager and the Son destined for center stage. No, Francis is telling us something different. His understanding of the Incarnation is more like a poem. God is a poet and the beauty of the poetry is expressed in the word that is spoken. Who can separate the poet from the poetry? Are they not, in some way, one and the same? So too when the Word becomes flesh, the Word does not say "good-bye" to the Father and take a plunge to earth. No, God—the Trinity of Father, Son and Spirit—becomes flesh in the person of Jesus. Listen again. The Father "announces" the Word. The Father expresses himself in the Son who is Word of the Father, and the relationship between them is manifested in the Spirit. Where the Son/Word is, so too is the Father and Spirit. The Trinity does not separate into parts in the Incarnation; rather, the entire Trinity is expressed in the person of Jesus Christ. When we consider this mystery, it is mind-boggling. The ineffable, transcendent, and utterly incomprehensible person of the Father comes to us in the poor and humble humanity of Christ. The source of all creation, the Most High good, comes to us in "the flesh of humanity and our frailty." The One who is so beyond our finite and limited minds takes on our poor and humble flesh without change, separation or confusion. There is no human reason that can understand this mystery, no logic, even no technology that can figure out this mystery of God. Only love can enter into the heart of the mystery.

The mystery of God as utterly transcendent and humbly present in fragile human flesh is a coincidence of opposites. In his masterful theological compendium, the *Breviloquium*, Bonaventure wrote that God is to be considered *altissime et piissime*, that is, God is to be considered "most lofty and most intimately" related to us.[29] It is not that God is lofty on one hand and intimately related on the other, it is, rather, that God's loftiness *is* God's intimacy. To live *in* the mystery of God is to live *in between* God's utter transcendence and God's personal embrace. God, we might say, is the incomprehensible One who is the breath of our lives, the utterly transcendent One who is the source of the universe and the One who personally loves each of us in a unique way.

Francis had insight into this mystery of God. Maybe because of his own experience of God in the church of San Damiano or maybe because of God's touch in his own life, Francis understood that God comes to us in a particular way, in the poverty and humility of Jesus Christ. His love of the poor is no secret to history. "To poor beggars," Bonaventure wrote, "he even wished to give not only his possessions but his very self"[30].... "In all the poor / [Francis] saw before him / a portrait of Christ."[31] Maybe because Francis was *not* an intellectual he could perceive the mystery of God in its pristine beauty—the extraordinary divine in the ordinary human. Too often we are wrapped up in lofty, intellectual speculations about God. We write books, use abstract language and complex philosophical terms to describe God. In the meantime, God is present to us not only in the mundane but in the poverty and humility of ordinary life. We do not usually gravitate to the poor and humble and therefore our heads are often in the clouds wondering whether or not God exists. If we truly recognized God in poor and humble fragile human flesh, we probably could not bear the weight of the mystery. We would find it overwhelming precisely because of its simplicity. However, this is the mystery of God that Francis perceived.

The simplest way to describe God's poverty and humility is in terms of love. Love gives itself away—this is God's poverty. Love turns toward the other so it can give itself to the other—this is God's humility. In the Incarnation, God turns toward us through the Son/Word and gives (him)self to us as love. We call this gift of God's love to us, this gift of total self-emptying love, "kenosis."[32] The poverty of God is the kenosis or self-emptying of the Word, the descent of the Word, from the riches of divine glory into our fragile human nature. The God whom Francis discovered is a God who shows himself to us in poor and humble fragile human flesh. This is a God who loves us so much as to be reckless in love; a God who throws it all away out of love and never tires of loving.

The humility of God makes people uneasy. It is not the way we normally think about God who we claim is almighty, all-powerful, all-knowing and everywhere present. The tile mosaic of the risen Christ in the Basilica of the Immaculate Conception in Washington, D.C., is closer to our idea of a mighty God: muscular, powerful, and in some ways looking like the "bionic man." But how does one portray a humble God? What images could we use to visualize a God of poor and humble love? It is difficult to conceive of God as humble. In fact, humility is what we usually ascribe to poor people ("they live in humble means"), demure people ("she is so humble, she never says a word"), those who are mentally challenged and anyone else who lives below cultural standards of wealth, health and success on every level. "Humility" is not a favorable word in our culture. To describe God as "humble" may seem outrageous or even scandalous. Who could stake one's life on a humble God? Yet, it was precisely the humility of God that caught Francis' attention—no, even better—to which he devoted his life. This is how Celano describes Francis:

> Humble in manner,
> he was more humble in opinion,
> and most humble in his own estimation.
> This *prince of God*
> could not be identified as a prelate,
> except by this sparkling gem:
> he was the least among the lesser.
> …There was no arrogance in his mouth,
> no pomp in his gestures,
> no conceit in his actions.
> He *learned* by revelation
> *the meaning* of many things,
> but when he was conversing among others
> he put the opinions of others ahead of his own.[33]

When we understand the God of poor and humble love then we understand Francis' poor and humble life. How can the lover be anything different from the beloved? The humility of God impressed Francis so much that he called himself a "brother minor," like Jesus. Francis encountered this mystery of God, in a special way, in the Eucharist, which he always called the "Body of Christ." In several of his writings on the Eucharist, he described humility as the "form" of God's presence to us in Jesus Christ. The revelation of God in the person of Jesus is expressed in humble form, ordinary form—bread—so ordinary that we eat it everyday without thinking twice because it is a basic means of nourishment. God comes to us in such an ordinary way that God is hidden to the spiritually blind and revealed only to those who can see with spiritual eyes. When the disciples asked Jesus why he spoke in parables, he replied: "that they may see but not perceive, / listen but not understand" (Luke 8:10). He went on to say, "when your eye is sound, your whole body too is filled with light, but when it is diseased your body too will be all darkness" (Luke 11:34).

Francis believed that the humility of God is apparent only to those who are living in "penance" or conversion, those who are striving to turn their hearts toward God and live in God. Such persons see with spiritual eyes. But those whose bodies are dark and diseased do not see properly and therefore the humble presence of God is hidden to them. It is to those who see with the eyes of the heart that the Father bends low in love and shows himself in the ordinary human flesh of the Son made visible to us by the Spirit. This is what Francis wrote in the first Admonition to his followers.

> The Lord Jesus says to his disciples: *I am the way, the truth and the life; no one comes to the Father except through me. If you knew me, you would also know my Father; and from now on, you do know him and have seen him. Philip says to him: Lord, show us the Father and it will be enough for us. Jesus says to him: Have I been with you for so long a time and you have not known me? Philip, whoever sees me sees my Father as well* [John 14:6–9].
>
> The Father dwells *in inaccessible light* [1 Timothy 6:16] and *God is Spirit* [John 4:24] and, *no one has ever seen God* [John 1:18]. Therefore He cannot be seen except in the Spirit because *it is the Spirit that gives life; the flesh has nothing to offer* [John 6:63]. But because He is equal to the Father, the Son is not seen by anyone other than the Father or other than the Holy Spirit.[34]

Here again Francis is captivated by the hiddenness of the Father in the Son. He calls us to "see" the presence of the Father in the Son, an "in-sight" which is made possible by the Spirit. It is the presence of the holy transcendent Father in the Son that renders the humanity of Christ more than mere flesh. As Francis claimed: "All who saw the Lord Jesus according to the humanity, therefore and did not see and believe according to the Spirit and the divinity that He is the true Son of God were condemned."[35] Fairly harsh words from a simple, peaceful man! What Francis wants us to grasp, however, is the profound truth of God's presence in ordinary flesh. He continues by saying, "as they saw only His flesh by an insight of their flesh, yet believed that God as they contemplated Him with their spiritual eyes, He was as we see bread and wine with our bodily eyes, let us see and firmly believe that they are His most holy Body and Blood living and true."[36] Thus, the Most High and holy One who is ultimate transcendent goodness is hidden in the ordinary things of this world, signified by bread and wine. As I recently saw on a local billboard for a Methodist church: "Coincidence means God chooses to remain anonymous."

The problem of "seeing" God's humility is that we are often blinded by a hardness of heart. The famous words of *The Little Prince* hold the same truth that Jesus shared with his disciples: "it is only with the heart that one can see rightly; what is essential is invisible to the eye."[37] If only we could see with the eyes of our hearts then we could behold each day the humility of God who comes to us, "appearing humbly" (Admonition 1:17). Joseph Kentenich, founder of the Schoenstatt movement, once said, "what you see and the way you love makes a difference. You can either increase the world's happiness or add to its sorrow."[38] Undoubtedly, what we see or the way we see influences our judgment of things. If we don't see clearly, it is because our vision is obstructed. Physical obstruction of the eyes, such as cataracts, causes everything to look blurry and out of focus. In the same way, the "cataracts of the heart" can cause everything to seem out of focus. People may look angry or mean to us and we say hurtful things in defense of our egos—"I am not talking to her because she ignored me" or "that person seems very unfriendly."

What Francis calls us to do is to look more deeply—first, within ourselves and then outside ourselves, at our brothers and sisters, our neighbors and all those we encounter—to look beneath the surface of the fragile flesh of the other into the depths of the reality before us. We cannot see clearly outwardly, however, unless we can see clearly inwardly. Only the pure of heart can see rightly, as Francis said in Admonition XVI: "The truly clear of heart are those who look down upon earthly things, seek those of heaven, and with a clean heart and spirit, never cease adoring and seeing the Lord God living and true."[39] Here is the great insight into living in relation to a humble God, a God who hides in ordinary human flesh. We cannot see God with our physical eyes nor can we find God through the logic of reason. The more we try to see God with our physical eyes or find God through logical analysis, the more we will fail. We will become increasingly frustrated and God will become more distant to us. To see the extraordinary ordinariness of God is to see with a different set of eyes, the eyes of the heart and to know God by a different logic, the logic of love. What Francis tells us in his Admonition is that we must contemplate the mystery of God. Contemplation takes place when we learn to see the mystery of God bent over in love in the fragile human flesh of Jesus Christ. The way to contemplate the mystery of God's humble love, according to Francis, is in the Eucharist. In his "Letter to the Entire Order" he beckons us to be attentive to the divine mystery:

> O wonderful loftiness and stupendous dignity!
> O sublime humility!
> O humble sublimity!
> The Lord of the universe,
> God and the Son of God,
> so humbles Himself
> that for our salvation
> He hides Himself
> under an ordinary piece of bread!
> Brothers, look at the humility of God,
> and *pour out your hearts before Him!*

Humble yourselves
that you may be exalted by Him!
Hold nothing back of yourselves for yourselves
that He Who gives Himself totally to you
may receive you totally![40]

Transcendence for Francis means "Holy Other" and immanence signifies the nearness of God. When Francis speaks of God's "sublimity and
humility" he is saying that the Holy Other is so foolishly near as to be
hidden in the most ordinary form—bread—the sacrament of fragile
human flesh. God hides in the simple, ordinary things of this world,
including our own lives! That is why everything radiates a tremendous
goodness beyond itself, because everything is imbued with the goodness of God.

But who could possibly behold the presence of the God of the universe in a little piece of ordinary bread? In Francis' view, it is the poor
person, the one who has space within one's heart to receive God. "Hold
back nothing of yourselves for yourselves," he said, "that he who gives
himself totally to you / may receive you totally."[41] The poor and humble person can see the poor and humble God in an ordinary piece of
bread. Those who are filled up with themselves have no room [or time]
for a humble God. They are so preoccupied with themselves—their
ideas, their greatness, their wealth and status—they cannot see beyond
their noses. Because they miss out on seeing God in the ordinary form
of bread or flesh, they confine God to the world of abstract ideas.
When we make God an idea and divorce God from concrete reality
then we become "gnostics" instead of Christians.[42]

Francis understood that God is not remote and distant, a God who
has nothing in common with creation. Rather, God is unstoppable
goodness—a God who simply can't wait to give everything away and
to love us where we are. God comes to us—that is God's humility—and
we are called to love him in return.

If God loves us where we are and comes to be with us humbly in
the flesh, then we must admit that the humility of God is intertwined
with the Incarnation. Incarnation we might say is God bending low to

embrace the world in love. This makes the entire creation—all peoples, all mountains and valleys, all creatures big and small, everything that exists—holy because God embraces it. This is what I believe Teilhard de Chardin was trying to tell us when he said, "There is nothing profane here below for those who have eyes to see."[43] Everything is sacred. The entire creation, including every person, is a sacrament of God because within each and every thing, in some way, God is hidden.

What Francis realized is that to see the humility of God in the world, one must live in the mystery of Christ. The humility of God is revealed in the humility of Christ. It is Christ who leads us into the mystery of God because Christ *is* the sacrament of God. We can only live in Christ, however, when we have the "Spirit of the Lord." "Desire above all else," Francis said, "to have the Spirit of the Lord."[44] The Spirit of the Lord enables us to penetrate the depths of created reality in which God is hidden, as Saint Paul writes, because "the Spirit reaches the depths of everything, even the depths of God" (1 Corinthians 2:11). What would the world be like if Christians actually *believed* in a humble God? If following a God of poverty and humility led them to abandon their opinions, prejudices and judgments so they could be more open to love others where they are, like God? Francis went about the world following the footprints of Christ, not so he could look like Christ, but because they were the footprints of divine humility. He discovered that God descends in love to meet us where we are and he found God in the most unexpected forms: the disfigured flesh of a leper, the complaints of a brother, the radiance of the sun, in short, the cloister of the universe. The wisdom of Francis makes us realize that God loves us in our incomplete humanity even though we are always running away trying to rid ourselves of defects, wounds and brokenness. If we could only see that God is there in the cracks of our splintered human lives we would already be healed.

The humility of God means acceptance—God accepts ordinary, fragile human flesh to reveal his glory so that we in turn may accept others as the revelation of God. Christ discloses the beauty of the world as the radiance of God. That is why every person and creature merits utmost respect and attention because in that living being, God dwells. We may be confounded by the mystery of God's humility if we try to understand it through reason alone. The humility of God is not an abstract concept. It is how God expresses himself in concrete reality. Francis teaches us that God is an inexhaustible mystery of love and we are invited to become like God, surrendered in love. We are invited to live in the humility of God and to see God's beauty in the heart of the world.

REFLECTION QUESTIONS
1. Where do you see yourself in relation to the humility of God?
2. Are you able to look at your life as the place where God's humble love dwells?
3. Can you see the humility of God in your community, your family, your coworkers? The poor and the sick?
4. What do you find most difficult in understanding the humility of God?

NOTES

[1] Pseudo-Dionysius (also known as Dionysius or Denis) was a monastic writer who probably lived in Syria around the year A.D. 500. Some claim he was the Athenian convert of Paul described in the Acts of the Apostles (17:34) and known as Dionysius the Areopagite. Others maintain that he was either Bishop Denis of Paris or the monophysite Patriarch Severus who assumed the pseudonym "Dionysius." Despite many attempts at identifying this figure, the historical personage remains a mystery. For a summary of Pseudo-Dionysius's writings and thought see Bernard McGinn, *The Foundations of Mysticism*, vol. 1, *The Presence of God: A History of Western Christian Mysticism* (New York: Crossroads, 1991), pp. 157–182; Andrew Louth, *The Origins of the Christian Mystical Tradition: From Plato to Denys* (New York: Oxford University Press, 1981), pp. 159–78.

[2] Augustine, *The Confessions of St. Augustine* 3.6.11, John Ryan, trans. (New York: Image Books, 1960), p. 84. Augustine writes: "But you were more inward than my inmost self, and superior to my highest being."

[3] "The Remembrance of the Desire of a Soul by Thomas of Celano in *Francis of Assisi: Early Documents*, volume II, *The Founder*, Regis J. Armstrong, J. A. Wayne Hellmann and William J. Short, eds. (New York: New City Press, 2000), p. 314, hereafter abbreviated as *FA:ED* II followed by page numbers.

[4] See Edouard d'Alençon, "Saint Françoise a-t-il existe?" *Etudes Franciscaines* 15 (1906): 481–495.

[5] Although Thomas of Celano wrote the first biography of Francis, Bonaventure's "official" biography of Francis was written at the request of the Franciscan Order because the Order was seeking consolidation and unity. For a brief history of this biography see the "introduction" to *The Legends and Sermons About Saint Francis by Bonaventure of Bagnoregio (1255–1267)*, in *FA:ED* II, pp. 495–505.

[6] "The Life of Saint Francis by Thomas of Celano," 1.2 in *Francis of Assisi: Early Documents*, volume 1, *The Saint*, Regis J. Armstrong, J.A. Wayne Hellmann and William J. Short, eds. (New York: New City Press, 1999), p. 183. This English edition of Francis' writings and the first life by Thomas of Celano will hereafter be referred to as *FA:ED* I, followed by page number.

[7] "The Life of Saint Francis by Thomas of Celano," 2.4 in *FA:ED* I, p. 185.

[8] "The Remembrance of the Desire of a Soul by Thomas of Celano," 6.10 in *FA:ED* II, p. 249.

[9] Bonaventure, "The Major Legend of Saint Francis," 1.5 in *FA:ED* II, p. 534.

[10] "The Remembrance of the Desire of a Soul by Thomas of Celano" 6.11 in *FA:ED* II, p. 250.

[11] Bonaventure, "The Major Legend of Saint Francis," 1.6 in *FA:ED* II, p. 534. The editors of this volume indicate that Bonaventure uses the word *compassio* five times in the text suggesting more than *miseratio* (an act of kindness) or *misericordia* (a heart sensitive to suffering). Compassion (*com-passio*) has the sense of suffering with another.

[12] Francis of Assisi, "Testament," 1–3 in *FA:ED* I, p. 124.

[13] "The Remembrance of the Desire of a Soul by Thomas of Celano," 124 in *FA:ED* II, p. 354.

[14] "The Life of Saint Francis by Thomas of Celano," 12 in *FA:ED* I, p. 210.

[15] Thadée Matura, *Francis of Assisi: The Message in His Writings*, Paul Barrett, trans. (New York: The Franciscan Institute, 1997), p. 53.

[16] Francis of Assisi, "Earlier Rule," 23.9 in *FA:ED* I, p. 85.

[17] Francis of Assisi, "Earlier Rule," 23.9 in *FA:ED* I, p. 85.

[18] Bonaventure, "The Major Legend of Saint Francis," 9.1 in *FA:ED* II, p. 596.

[19] Francis of Assisi, "Earlier Rule" 23.11 in *FA:ED* I, pp. 85–86.

[20] Norbert Nguyên-Van-Khanh, *The Teacher of His Heart: Jesus Christ in the Thought and Writings of St. Francis* (New York: The Franciscan Institute, 1994), pp. 91–150.

[21] Thadée Matura, "'My Holy Father!' God as Father in the Writings of St. Francis," *Greyfriars Review* 1 (1987): 105–129.

[22] Francis of Assisi, "A Letter to the Entire Order," 51–52 in *FA:ED* I, pp. 120–121.

[23] Matura, *Francis of Assisi*, p. 82.

[24] Francis of Assisi, "Earlier Rule" 23.1; "A Letter to the Entire Order," p. 50.

[25] Francis of Assisi, "Earlier Rule," 23.3 in *FA:ED* I, pp. 81–82.

[26] Bonaventure, *Breviloquium*, 5.8 (V, 261).

[27] For a discussion of *eros* and *agape* see Anders Nygren, *Agape and Eros*, Philip S. Watson, trans. (Philadelphia: Westminster, 1953).

[28] Francis of Assisi, "Later Admonition and Exhortation," 4–5 in *FA:ED* I, p. 46.

[29] Bonaventure, *Breviloquium*, 1.2 (V, 211).

[30] Bonaventure, "The Major Legend of Saint Francis," 1.6 in *FA:ED* II, p. 534.

[31] Bonaventure, "The Major Legend of Saint Francis" 8.5 in *FA:ED* II, p. 589.

[32] For a definition of *kenosis* see Sarah Coakley, "Kenosis: Theological Meanings and Gender Connotations," in *The Work of Love: Creation as Kenosis*, John Polkinghorne, ed. (Grand Rapids, Mich.: William B. Eerdmans, 2001), pp. 193–194. The classic kenotic text in the New Testament is Philippians 2:1–11, referring to Christ who "emptied (*ekenosen*) himself, taking the form of a servant."

[33] "The Remembrance of the Desire of a Soul by Thomas of Celano," 102 in *FA:ED* II, p. 338.

[34] Francis of Assisi, "Admonition I," 1–7 in *FA:ED* I, p. 128.

[35] Francis of Assisi, "Admonition I," 8 in *FA:ED* I, p. 128.

[36] Francis of Assisi, "Admonition I," 20–21 in *FA:ED* I, p. 129.

[37] Antoine de Saint Exupéry, *The Little Prince*, Katherine Woods, trans. (New York: Harcourt Brace Jovanovich, 1971), p. 87.

[38] Joseph Kentenich, cited in Ann W. Astell, introduction to *Divine Representations: Postmodern Spirituality* (New York: Paulist, 1994), p. 8.

[39] Francis of Assisi, "Admonition XVI," in *FA:ED* I, p. 134.

[40] Francis of Assisi, "A Letter to the Entire Order," 27–29 in *FA:ED* I, p. 118.

[41] Francis of Assisi, "A Letter to the Entire Order," 27–29 in *FA:ED* I, p. 118.

[42] Gnosticism was a heresy of the early church that advocated dualism (light/darkness, good/evil) and a spiritual understanding of God that divorced God from a finite, mutable world. For a summary of Gnosticism see Robert Grant, "Gnostic Spirituality," in *Christian Spirituality: Origins to the Twelfth Century*, ed. Bernard McGinn and John Meyendorff, vol. 1, *World Spirituality: An Encyclopedic History of the Religious Quest*, Ewert Cousins, ed. (New York: Crossroad, 1987), pp. 44–60.

[43] Pierre Teilhard de Chardin, *The Divine Milieu: An Essay on the Interior Life*, William Collins, trans. (New York: Harper and Row, 1960), p. 66.

[44] Francis of Assisi, "Later Rule," 10.8 in *FA:ED* I, p. 105.

Chapter Two

THE HUMBLE HEART OF GOD

It is love who mixed the mortar
And it's love who stacked these stones
And it's love that made the stage here
Though it looks like we're alone
In this scene set in shadows
Like the night is here to stay
There is evil cast around us
But it's love that wrote the play
In this darkness
Love can show the way
—David Wilcox, "Show the Way"

hen we talk about the humility of God we are really talking about two profound mysteries: the Trinity and Christ. We cannot separate these mysteries without doing damage to both of them. The Trinity without Christ is mere speculation and Christ without the Trinity is absurd—a dead man raised from the dead and still living. Francis of Assisi seemed to have no problem in holding these two mysteries together. In fact, for him they were so intertwined that one led to the other. To grasp more fully the mystery of the humility of God, however, we must examine the Trinity and Christ separately to see how they relate to one another.

In order to gain insight to the nature of God as Trinity, it is helpful to turn to the Franciscan theologian, Bonaventure of Bagnoregio.

Unlike Francis, Bonaventure was a trained theologian, having studied under the renowned master Alexander of Hales at the University of Paris in the thirteenth century. He was quite familiar with the classical tradition of theology including Augustine, Bernard, the Victorines and the Greek philosophers Plato and Aristotle. However, he was equally impressed by Francis' own life and intuitions and we find many of Francis' themes on goodness, the cross and Trinity in the writings of Bonaventure. At a fairly young age, Bonaventure had to leave his budding academic career at the university to become the seventh Minister General of the Franciscan Order because of a crisis within the Order. He held this position for about seventeen years. I believe his years of guiding the Franciscans, who were dealing with various problems in the Order, as well as in the church, helped shape his theology in a way that differed from other scholastic theologians, including his contemporary Thomas Aquinas.

Like Francis, Bonaventure looked to the Incarnation as the embodiment of God rather than a peculiarly Christian understanding of God. Incarnation means that God takes on flesh. Jesus is the Word-made-flesh, a Word from which we could read the ultimate nature of God and of human nature itself. Bonaventure wrote that God could not communicate himself to another, that is, the Incarnation could not take place, if God were not infinitely communicative in himself. This makes sense. How could God share himself in the form of a human person if the nature of God did not have the capacity to give itself away? Here is a simple example: A woman cannot naturally conceive a child alone; it is physically impossible. She has the capacity to conceive, however, through intimate relationship with another but she cannot do so without the other. In the same way God could not communicate himself to a finite other if he did not have the capacity to communicate within himself. So, Bonaventure concluded, God cannot be a monad, a single, isolated, individual one. There must be plurality within God. God must be Trinity.

Bonaventure's theology of the Trinity was influenced by two major writers in the tradition, Pseudo-Dionysius and Richard of St. Victor, a twelfth-century Victorine writer. Following Pseudo-Dionysius, Bonaventure considered the name of God in the Old Testament as being: "I AM WHO AM" (Exodus 3:14). In the New Testament, however, God reveals himself as Good: "No one is good but God alone" (Luke 18:19).[1] Bonaventure identified goodness as the name of God and looked to Pseudo-Dionysius and Richard of St. Victor to understand God as ultimate goodness. According to Pseudo-Dionysius, the highest good is self-diffusive and gives rise to being.[2] Richard claimed that the highest good is love, and love is personal and communicative.[3] According to Richard, charity, which is the supreme form of the good, is the basis for showing the necessity of a plurality of persons in the Godhead. Since charity necessarily involves a relation to another, there can be no charity where there is no plurality. Charity must be in proportion to the good that is loved. The perfect communication of love, according to Richard, must involve no less than three persons.[4] Zachary Hayes summarizes his position as follows:

> If there were only one person in God, then a perfect self-communication would not be possible at all; for no creature could sustain such a communication. So, there must be at least two persons in God; there must be a perfectly lovable other. But if there were only two, then there could only be their love for one another; and this would not be the fullness of love. For if love by nature involves a relation to another, the highest perfection of love demands that each of the two persons in love share that love with yet another. Hence, Richard argues that there must be in God not only a *dilectum* but a *condilectum* as well. Condilectio is found where a third is loved by two in harmony.[5]

It is from these relationships of love that Bonaventure began to consider the divine persons of the Trinity. He used the notion of self-diffusive goodness and personal love to distinguish the persons of the Trinity as a communion of persons-in-love. Here is where we must engage more deeply in the mystery of the Trinity if we are to understand the humble heart of God.

According to Bonaventure, the Father is the source or fountain fullness of infinite goodness because the Father is primal and self-diffusive.[6] The person of the Father is the source of the other two divine persons because the Father is without origin or beginning. The name "Father," therefore, does not mean that God is male or Jewish but it refers to that person who is the infinite source of goodness. An image of the Father to help us appreciate the first person of the Trinity is that of waterfalls. Anyone who has ever seen the torrents of gushing waters bursting forth over Niagara Falls has never failed to gasp in awe and wonder at the magnificent power of these waters. Imagine that the source of these bursting torrents of waters is infinite. Such an image, although a limited one, gives us an idea of what the Father's infinite goodness is like.

As the Father's goodness diffuses forth, it diffuses in a personal way to a personal other and that is the Son. The Son is that person eternally generated by the Father's self-diffusive goodness, the total personal expression of the Father. The Son is everything the Father is in one other than the Father. So the Son is the perfect image of the Father. Now here is an important point for Bonaventure. Because the Son is the total expression of the Father, the Son is *Word*.[7] The Word is the otherness of the Father, the complete expression of the mystery of God, who, while God, is other than the Father.[8] The Word is a permanent and unchanging self-expression of the Father that cannot be separated from the Father. Since the Father is eternal and eternally expressive, the Son/Word is also eternal and eternally expressed. The Father and Son/Word are so intimately united with one another that they breathe forth love in a single will, the love of the Spirit. The Spirit is that freedom-in-love between the Father and Son that completes their love in a holy and eternal union.

We are at this point pondering the "inner life" of God, as if entering into the awesome mystery of three divine persons in love. If we find this divine life too lofty to ponder, we can lower the bar of imagination one notch and think of our own lives. Think of someone you truly love or have loved. What is the power of that love that draws you to that person? Do you love that person because you have to or because you want to? Does the attraction of love with that person draw you beyond yourself in such a way that if you stopped loving that person, something real and tangible would die, perhaps the spiritual bond of love between you? If you have had an experience of love, then you have had some insight into the Trinity of love. In fact, by loving another person you have been—yes, believe it or not—caught up in the Trinity of love. The Trinity is not three men at a tea party. It is a mystery of relationships—giving, receiving and sharing love. When we say "God is love" we are saying that God is a mystery of persons-in-love.

Love brought this creation into being. Do you believe that? Or do you think it is simply a nice, "feel-good" statement? When we say "God is love" are we merely saying something *nice* about God or something that speaks to us about who God is? Is the statement "God is love" based on the revelation of God in Jesus Christ or something Saint John the Evangelist felt like saying because he was having a good day? Again, I ask you, what forms your image(s) of God? It is an important question because we cannot pray to a loving God or say "God is love" and then go about the world as if God is entirely something other than love. When we say "God is love" we are either saying something about who God is or we are merely reciting empty, although pious, words. Now, hopefully, you will agree with me (as with Bonaventure) that when we say "God is love" we are saying something not only about *who* God is but *what* God is. We can draw an analogy to human relations. When we describe a person as good "she is so good"—we are saying something not only about the person but we are saying *what* the person is, based on our experience. Just as we can experience the goodness of another person, so, too, we can experience God as love, because this is how God reveals himself to us. The experience of love tells us that love can never be isolated or individual, love needs to be shared. The nature of God is to share love and that is why the word "God" cannot be abstract, devoid of meaning or individualized because the word "God" means relationship, a communion of persons-in-love. God is Trinity.

Love cannot exist in isolation or autonomously because love shares itself with another. Love requires a lover and a beloved, a giver and a receiver. It is the receptivity of love that makes it gift. The Father who is the fountain fullness of love is always moving toward the Son in the sharing of love, and this sharing of love is the Spirit. This eternal movement of the Father toward the Son—this continuous, dynamic, outpouring of self-diffusive love—indicates to us that God not only shares love but God shares love completely. Whatever God gives, Bonaventure said, God gives completely.[9] In chapter one, we spoke of "kenosis" or self-emptying. We might say that kenosis takes place in the Trinity, in the self-communicative love of the Father to the Son. Because there is a type of self-emptying of the Father in the eternal generation of the Son, we can say that God is poor and humble by nature. In this divine infinite life, which far exceeds the boundaries of our small, finite imaginations, the Father communicates love in such a personal and total way that the Father is turned, by nature, toward the Son/Word. The complete self-gift of the Father to the Son is the Father's "poverty." Perhaps the Father could have had a different relation to the Son. If the Father was an introverted being who liked to think and share his ideas, he could have done so in relation to the Son without ever really fully expressing himself or giving himself away. But this is not the Father of self-diffusive goodness/self-communicative love. No, the Father of overflowing love is unstoppable goodness, overflowing into the other, the Son. The turning of the Father toward the Son is the Father's humility. Humility is not a quality of God, it is the essence of God as love. The Son is the object of the Father's love and yet loves the Father so completely as to breathe forth love in the Spirit. The Son is the heart of the Trinity and the center between the Father and Spirit, receiving love from the Father and loving with the Father in a single breath of love, which is the Spirit. Imagine this dancing swirl of persons-in-love, almost like the dervish of the Sufi mystics. It is a continuous, dynamic, overflowing and outward movement of love.

Where do we stand, we finite created beings, with regard to this generous, overflowing God of love? What is our place in this divine mystery? Perhaps we may think of ourselves as isolated on planet Earth, waiting for this God of love to come and rescue us. Or perhaps we may imagine this God of love as a small elite community that we would like to join but are unsure about membership. These ideas, of course, are incorrect. For Bonaventure, we are right there in the heart of the mystery, each one of us and all creation, caught up in the love of the Father and Son. It seems incredible but if we follow the logic of these Trinitarian relationships, we will see that we are enveloped in the infinite love of the Trinity. God is so close to us that we don't even recognize the awesome mystery in which we are caught up. As Bonaventure once wrote, "I know myself better in God than in myself."[10]

To understand our relation to this God of infinite, dancing love, we need to take a closer look at the relationship between the Father and Son, because it is within this relationship that we find our meaning, purpose and goal of life. The Father, as we said before, is completely self-expressive by the nature of self-communicative love. The word "ex-press" means a "pressing outward." All that the Father is, all his divine ideas, which are no different from the Father's love, (in other words, the Father doesn't "think" on one hand and "love" on the other) are "projected outwards" and "im-pressed" (so to speak) in the Son. We may use the analogy of language here. If the Father is the "thought," the Son, who is Word, is the thought expressed. This idea is not far from what Francis was trying to articulate in his "Later Admonition and Exhortation" when he described the Incarnation as the announcement of the Word by the Father. The Father is the one who speaks, the Word is that which is spoken and the Spirit is what unites the one who speaks with that which is spoken. What is important to keep in mind here is that the Word (of God) does not exist as a self-sufficient entity but precisely as the Word or expression of the Father.

When we say "all things are created through the Word" (John 1:3), we are saying that the Father expresses himself in the Son and this self-expression is the basis of the infinite Word of God and all finite existence as well. Creation, as a "coming into existence," emerges in this relationship between the Father and Son. Creation is a finite expression of the infinite Word of God. It is caught up in the mystery of the generation of the Word from the Father and is generated out of the fecundity of God's love. Here perhaps is the most important point with regard to our relationship to God and God's relationship to us. To be created does not mean some divine magical trick by which God makes things appear out of nothing. God is not a magician. Nor does creation mean that the Trinity had a meeting and decided that it would be more inclusive and have finite beings participate in its membership. The Trinity is not a town council. Creation does not mean that God is a retired potter and we are lovely clay pots for display. We are not God's amusement or entertainment. Nor was God depressed when he decided to do something new and came up with the idea of creation. We are simply not a novelty to make God happy, as if God might not be eternally happy being a community of love. In whatever image we have of ourselves and God, we must rid ourselves of the idea that God is somewhere "out there" and we are here on this little planet Earth, in a valley of tears, waiting to be saved from a treacherous fate beyond our control. This is not the God of love who has been revealed to us in Christ.

If we really believe that God *is* love and this love is the love of the Father for the Son united in the Spirit, then we must also believe that we are part of this wonderful, awesome, incredible relationship of love. Creation is not a mere external act of God, an object on the fringe of divine power. Rather, it is rooted in the self-diffusive goodness of God's inner life and emerges out of the innermost depths of Trinitarian life.[11] This means that creation emanates out of and is a limited expression of divine goodness. We are not outside God as if God lives in a mansion surrounded by pearly gates. We are not separated from God by space and time, wondering what will become of us after death if we are not saved. If the lover were to distance himself from the beloved, the beloved would perish from lack of love. So, too, if we emerge out of the loving relationship between the Father and Son, then it is indeed love that has brought us (and continues to bring us) into being. Without the source of love that sustains us, God's love, we would die. And it is precisely because of this relationship that we must abandon any spatial-temporal ideas of God that distance God from us. We must come to perceive that we, created, finite beings, unfold "within" the Trinitarian relations of divine love. We are immersed, in a finite way, in the infinite love of God. It is in light of this idea that the words of the prophet Isaiah speak to us: "I have called you by your name, you are mine. / Should you pass through the sea, I will be with you;

/ or through rivers, they will not swallow you up. / Should you walk through fire, you will not be scorched / and the flames will not burn you. / For I am Yahweh, your God" (Isaiah 43:2–3).

How did we come to be caught up in this wonderful, infinite relationship of divine love? In Bonaventure's view, we are caught up in this mystery because we share an integral relation to the divine Word of God. God utters each one of us as a little word, Thomas Merton writes, as a partial thought of himself.[12] That is why when the Word became flesh, there was a real "fit" between the divine nature and created human nature to receive the divine Word. From the "beginning," creation has had the capacity to receive God into it because it is a finite expression of the infinite Word of God. Zachary Hayes writes, "when God creates, he can do so only in and through the Word of His own otherness, so that whatever created reality exists appears as the external otherness that is placed through the immanent otherness. Creation, therefore, in its inner constitution possesses a relation to the uncreated Word of God."[13] Creation finitely expresses the infinite love of the Father for the Son in the Spirit. While the Word is the full, immanent expression of all that the Father is in one who is other than the Father, the world is the external expression of the immanent Word.[14]

From its very existence, creation has been ready to receive the divine Word into it because it is created through the Word and in a finite way expresses the Word. If every created thing expresses the Word, then we would have to say that, in some way, all of creation is incarnational. That is why when the Word was made flesh there was a perfect fit between divine and human natures because the whole time of creation up until the Incarnation was prepared to receive the fullness of the Word into it. The Word of God "links" the Trinity and creation. Just as the Word is the otherness of the Father, we might say that creation is the otherness of God because of its intimate relation to the Word of God. We are not little creatures who live down below in the valley of earth. We are created lovers of God and even though we are finite and incomplete in our loving relationship with God, we are caught up in the eternal love of the Father and Son. It is from the Word that all creation flows, and it is to the Word, as exemplar, that it reflects back and returns.[15] Because of the centrality of the Word, creation takes place and flourishes within the divine life.[16]

I know you will ask, if we are so caught up in this eternal love affair of the Trinity, why is it that we suffer in this world, that people die and things change, that everything seems to pass away? The answer is not simple but is related to the fact that we are finite beings and radically dependent on God. Being finite, we are subject to change because what is finite does not last forever. Only love endures. So, if you really want to know how you and I (and the world) "fit" into this drama of divine love, you must pray. Only a relationship of love with God can lead you into the heart of God. There you will discover a little of the great mystery that is your life. As we read in Psalm 34: "Everyone separated from Love is empty and hungry within; But those who open their hearts to the Beloved, are filled to overflowing!"[17]

The mystery of God, at times, seems so lofty and beyond our ability to understand it; yet, it really lies within the human heart because the human heart dwells in and reflects the heart of God. The great spiritual writer Henri Nouwen captured the mystery of our lives caught up in the great mystery of God's love when he wrote:

> Do not hesitate to love and to love deeply....
> The more you have loved and have allowed yourself to
> suffer
> Because of your love,
> The more you will be able
> To let your heart grow
> Wider and deeper.[18]

This, I believe, is what the mystery of God's love is like, ever-deepening love. Within that loving embrace of God, our lives are brought into being and sustained in being. As we have been loved into birth, so, too, we are called to mirror God's love for others so as to birth God anew in creation. For that is how God, the tremendous lover of life, delights in his creation.

REFLECTION QUESTIONS

1. How do you see God's special love for you?
2. What are some of your common images of God? How do they shape your understanding of God's presence in the world?
3. How do you understand the words: "I have called you by name and you are mine" (Isaiah 43:3)?
4. What does it mean to "live in the Trinity?" How does living in the Trinity give purpose to your life?
5. What does it mean to you to be a "little word" uttered by God?

NOTES

[1] The comparison between John Damascene and Pseudo-Dionysius on the names of God as Being and Good are discussed by Bonaventure in his classic *Itinerarium Mentis in Deum*. See Bonaventure, *Itinerarium Mentis in Deum* (Itin.) 5.2 (V, 307).

[2] Pseudo-Dionysius *De divinis nominibus* 4.1 (PG 3, 694). For an excellent discussion of the tradition see Ewert H. Cousins, "The Notion of the Person in the *De Trinitate* of Richard of St. Victor," (unpublished Ph. D. dissertation, Fordham University, 1966).

[3] Richard of St. Victor *De Trinitate*, 3.14–19 (PL 196, pp. 924–927).

[4] See Zachary Hayes, introduction to *Disputed Questions on the Mystery of the Trinity*, vol. 3, *Works of Saint Bonaventure*, George Marcil, ed. (New York: The Franciscan Institute, 1979), pp. 15–16.

[5] Hayes, introduction to *Disputed Questions*, pp. 16–17.

[6] Bonaventure, I *Sentence* (Sent.). d. 27, p.1, a. un., q. 2, ad 3 (I, 470). The idea that the Father is *innascible* (not born) and fecund underlies the dialectical style of Bonaventure's thought. It also provides the basis of Bonaventure's metaphysics as a "coincidence of opposites." The Father's innascibility and fecundity are mutually complementary opposites, which cannot be formally reduced to one or the other; the Father is generative because he is unbegotten. See Hayes, introduction to *Disputed Questions*, p. 42, n. 51.

[7] Bonaventure, I *Sent*. d. 5, a. 1, q. 2, resp. (I, 115); I *Sent*. d. 2, a. u., q. 4, fund 2 (I, 56); Hayes, introduction to *Disputed Questions*, p. 34, n. 10. Bonaventure uses the terms *per modum naturae* and *per modum voluntatis* to designate the two trinitarian emanations of Son and Spirit respectively. The terms are inspired by Aristotle's principle that there exist only two perfect modes of production; namely, natural and free.

[8] Zachary Hayes, commentary on "Sermon II on the Nativity of the Lord," in *What Manner of Man?*, p. 80 n. 14.

[9] Bonaventure, *Itin*. 6.3 (V, 311).

[10] Bonaventure, *Hexaëmeron* (Hex.) 12.9 (V, 386).

[11] For Bonaventure's view on Trinity and creation see Delio, *Simply Bonaventure*, pp. 54–64.

[12] Thomas Merton, *New Seeds of Contemplation* (New York: New Directions Books, 1961), p. 37.

[13] Zachary Hayes, "Incarnation and Creation in St. Bonaventure," in *Studies Honoring Ignatius Brady, Friar Minor*, Romano Stephen Almagno and Conrad L. Harkins, eds. (New York: The Franciscan Institute, 1976), p. 315.

[14] Hayes, "Incarnation and Creation," p. 322.

[15] Ewert Cousins, "The Two Poles of Bonaventure's Thought," *Sancta Bonaventura 1274–1974*, vol. 4, Jacques-Guy Bougerol, ed. (Grottaferatta: Collegii S. Bonaventurae, 1974), p. 161.

[16] Denis Edwards, *The God of Evolution* (New York: Paulist, 1999), p. 30.

[17] Nan C. Merrill, *Psalms For Praying* (New York: Continuum, 2000), p. 60.

[18] Henri J.M. Nouwen, *The Inner Voice of Love: A Journey Through Anguish to Freedom* (New York: Doubleday, 1996), p. 59.

Chapter Three

GOD HUMBLY BENDS DOWN

Jesus and his disciples left for the villages round Caesarea Philippi. On the way he put this question to his disciples, "Who do people say I am?" And they told him. "John the Baptist," they said "others Elijah; others again, one of the prophets." "But you," he asked "who do you say I am?"
—Mark 8:27–29

It is without doubt that every person who knows something of the great Christian story knows something about Adam and Eve. Adam and Eve lived in a lovely garden until one day the Evil One appeared. The Evil One tempted Eve to eat of the forbidden tree and from that moment on humanity was doomed to death and separated from God. The story continues that while God was angry, hurt and disappointed at Eve and Adam's choice of eating fruit from the forbidden tree, God did not completely abandon them. Instead, several thousand years later, God sent his only Son, Jesus Christ, to save fallen humankind from sin and death. Jesus was born, lived a brief life, died by public execution on a cross and reconciled all men and women to God. At Easter Christians sing, "O Happy Fault!" because if Eve had not eaten the forbidden fruit, luring Adam and his descendents into a perilous death, Christ would not have come. The whole point of Jesus, according to the story, is based on the wrong choices of finite human beings.

While this story of the Incarnation lingered around for centuries, it became a significant part of the Christian tradition only after the eleventh century and Anselm of Canterbury's famous work, *Why the God-Man?* Jesus came, Anselm said, to repay the debt due to sin. However, not every thinker in the tradition believed that Jesus came only to pay sin's debt. Some early writers like Irenaeus of Lyons (approximately A.D. 200) or Maximus the Confessor (approximately A.D. 600) saw the Incarnation more as the completion of the cosmos rather than a payback for sin or a cure for illness. This idea, too, was shared among Franciscan writers as well.[1]

In the Middle Ages the tendency of theologians was to move from the story of Jesus to the widest possible horizon. They developed a style of reflection that today is commonly called "cosmic Christology." This means looking out at the entire world as one sees it at a particular time and trying to perceive the possible relations between the story of Jesus and the larger picture of the world.[2] The idea of cosmic Christology was already rooted in New Testament writers such as John the Evangelist and Paul who saw the immense significance in the life of Jesus, far more than one human being's life. In the opening of his Gospel, John pointed to the intrinsic connection between the mystery of creation and the mystery of Incarnation. "In the beginning was the Word," John writes, "Through him all things came to be, not one thing had its being but through him" (John 1:1–3).

For the Franciscan theologians, the life of Jesus provided a divine clue as to the structure and meaning not only of humanity but of the entire universe.[3] The thirteenth-century philosopher Duns Scotus said that the Incarnation was too great a mystery to simply remedy a defect. Rather, from all eternity, Christ was willed by God to come in the highest glory. The reason, according to Scotus, is simply that God is love and wanted to love a creature who could fully respond in love. Christ would have come, he said, even if there had been no sin. Christ is the first in God's intention to love and it is because of Christ that creation has its meaning. The Franciscan scholar Bill Short aptly states, "why build the Taj Majal to cover a pothole?"[4] Indeed, why would so great an event as the Incarnation, the Word become flesh, occur only *after* humans sinned? Why would so great and glorious an event happen because of a *defect* in humanity?

In the Franciscan view, the Incarnation occurs because of a

positive—love—not a negative—sin. This is an important point because the way we understand the Incarnation shapes our lives as Christians in the world. If love *is* the reason for the Incarnation then it is also the reason for God's humility because, as we saw in Francis, God's love is a humble love. It is a love that goes out of itself toward the other for the sake of the other. In his "Sermon on the Nativity of the Lord" Bonaventure captured the core of the humility of God when he wrote: "'The Word was made flesh' [John 1:14]. These words give expression to that heavenly mystery... that *the eternal God has humbly bent down* and lifted the dust of our nature into unity with his own person."[5] For Bonaventure, Incarnation signifies a God who humbly bends down to lift us up. Humility means that God is turned toward us just as the Father is turned toward the Son in love. Because we are finite creatures, God bends over in love to embrace us.

The idea of "bending over" or "bending down" reminds me of the days when I took care of my nephew when he was just a baby. I recall moments when I would see him lying in his oversized crib—a tiny creature with hands and feet waving in the air, totally helpless. I would bend down into the crib and lift him high up in the air and he would smile uncontrollably, as only an infant can. The humility of God is something like the baby in the crib. God is at once the small helpless infant who lies quietly in the crib of the universe, and also the strong one who can raise up a fragile human being and draw that person into the embrace of infinite love. God is Most High and Most Humble. I must admit that I am attracted to the idea of Incarnation as "God bending low." Whereas the Trinity is the dancing circle of love, the Incarnation is the profound bow of God stretching forth the divine arms in a wide embrace of love. God not only loves creation profoundly but the "bow" is holy and reverential, as if God loves us to such an extent that he reverences every aspect of creation. God bends low so that God can meet us exactly where we, finite, fragile, created human beings, creatures and all living things, are. God bends low because we are small, limited, frail, confused, bewildered, chaotic and sometimes just plain infantile. God bends low because God's arms are much longer than ours, and God reaches out for our tiny human hands. Imagine a God who is humbly bent low to embrace us in love compared to a God who sits high above on a throne and keeps score of human sins. Imagine a God who is so great in love that God desires to share love with fragile and incomplete human beings compared to a God who loves only himself and wants to glorify himself by creating finite creatures to glorify him even though they have a hard time because they are full of defects due to sin. What Bonaventure (like Francis) realized in the mystery of the Incarnation is that God bends over in love to meet us where we are. God is Most High and most intimately related to us.

If God is love and love renders God a Trinity of persons-in-love then it is difficult to conceive of a God who judges harshly or unfairly or metes out undue punishment because of human bad behavior. Rather, as Saint Paul writes:

> Love is always patient and kind; it is never jealous; love is never boastful or conceited; it is never rude or selfish; it does not take offence, and is not resentful. Love takes no pleasure in other people's sins but delights in the truth; it is always ready to excuse, to trust, to hope, and to endure whatever comes. Love does not come to an end. (1 Corinthians 13:4–8)

If God is love and it is love that brings us to birth, then it is difficult to conceive of the Incarnation, the Word made flesh, in any other way but the way of love. Love is what brought this creation into being and love is what will bring creation to its fulfillment to celebrate and participate in the eternal love of the Trinity. How love completes that which is brought into being is the story of Jesus, is the story of us humans, and is the story of the whole evolutionary creation itself. Jesus, the Trinity of love, and the universe story belong together.

We could easily get lost, however, in this love story between God and creation if we did not keep in mind the *humility* of God's love. We might imagine a love feast where everyone is happy and embracing one another. When Bonaventure speaks of the humility of God, he is saying that God not only meets us where we are but God meets us where we are in our sinfulness, our ugliness, our violent tendencies and selfish behaviors. The humility of God means that God's love is so abundant that God is willing to plunge into the darkness of humanity to bring us into the fullness of life. That is why God's humility is expressed most vividly in the cross because God could not bend over any further in love for us than in the suffering and death of the cross. In a small work called *The Tree of Life* Bonaventure depicted the passion of Christ in graphic images in order to convey the depths of God's humble love. The Beloved, he said, appeared on the cross stripped and bruised like a leper in order to invite us to join with him in this passion of love. Bonaventure writes:

> For crowned with thorns
> he was ordered to bend his back
> under the burden of the cross
> and to bear his own ignominy.
> Led to the place of execution,
> he was stripped of his garments
> so that he seemed to be a leper
> from the bruises and cuts in his flesh
> that were visible over his back and sides
> from the blows of the scourges
> And then transfixed
> with nails,
> he appeared to you as your beloved
> ...Who will grant me
> that my request should come about
> and that God will give me
> what I long for, that
> ...I may be fixed with my beloved
> to the yoke of the cross?[6]

What Bonaventure points out is that the cross reveals the mystery of God's overflowing love. Unlike finite human love that draws up conditions for its wants and needs, God's love is unconditional and totally self-giving. God humbly bends down to the lowest possible level to be God "for us" even in our weaknesses. The dereliction of the cross is the most intense revelation of the divine humility. The piercing of the human heart of Christ is the opening up of the depth of divine love embodied in the love of the Son of God.[7] Jesus was not just another good man who died for a noble cause. Jesus was the Son of God who died that we may have life and have it to the full—and we are called to follow him. This life given to us in abundance in and through the death of Jesus, is grounded in the humility of God's love. In Bonaventure's view, the mystery of cruciform love leads us into the very heart of the mystery of God.[8]

How do we come to know this God of humble love? Like Francis, Bonaventure claimed that we come to know the humility of God through Jesus. Bonaventure used the metaphor of the "book" to describe Jesus as the revelation of God. Jesus is the "Book of Life," the book written within in his divinity and without in his humanity. Jesus is the "Book of Life" because Jesus is the *Word of God*. The humanity of Christ is not a second word related to an inner (divine) word, according to Bonaventure, but is precisely the form the Word of God takes when it is expressed externally. Because Jesus is the book written within and without one could find in this book everything he or she wants to know about life—the basic law of created reality, the reason for being human, as well as the basic insights of the nature of God. By reading this book, Bonaventure claimed, we could come to know God's humility and poverty, which leads one into the heart of God.

Although Jesus is *the* book, creation is a "book" of God as well. In fact it was the first book, Bonaventure said, we humans were supposed to read in order to know God. Francis of Assisi, after taking up a life of conversion, was able to read the "Book of Creation" in his own way. Bonaventure said "in beautiful things, he saw Beauty itself."[9] Thomas of Celano wrote, "he spares lanterns, lamps, and candles unwilling to use his hand to put out their brightness which is a sign of the *eternal light*. He walked reverently over rocks, out of respect for Him who is called *the Rock*."[10] Bonaventure claimed that we should have been able to know God through the "Book of Creation" but our vision became poor due to sin; the Book of Creation became illegible. However, when Christ came the Book of Creation and the Book of Life became two volumes bound in one, so to speak. Christ is *the* Book of Life. Somehow we still do not read this book properly. We buy lots of books hoping to find the answers to our many questions of life; yet, we do not know how to read this "Book of Life," the "Book of Christ."

What does it require to read a book? It requires time, quiet, patience, attentiveness to the written words, imagination and emotions. Reading a book, if it is a good book, should move us from one level of life to another because once the mind is moved to insight and the heart is changed, life is never the same. Reading a good book is experiential. It is living in the drama of someone else's life or it may be allowing the drama of the story to touch one's own life. The two stories—the story of the book and the history of the reader—merge. The horizon of the book and the horizon of the reader become one and a new horizon emerges, the horizon of insight or a new understanding of life.

This is how we should read the Book of Life, in a way that we come to a new horizon of life, new insight. But few people read this book with any imagination. Nor does the book seem to move a whole lot of people to new levels of insight. The world would be quite different if it did. Many people hear the Scriptures read on Sunday but hearing the same stories read over and over again seems to make little difference to anyone. The words come and go in the same way that people say, "have a nice day," and move on. There are many Christians who mistake ritual for worship, attending Mass for listening to the gospel and reading the Book of Life. Oftentimes the worship of God is empty even though people seem to be present for the ritual. No wonder we have a difficult time finding God in our world. We search and search for God, spend lots of energy trying to reason and speculate about God, but often our search seems to be in vain—we simply cannot find God—and sometimes we give up the search because we are too weary to continue.

And yet, the search for God, the clues to God's presence in the universe, are given to us in the Book of Life—the Book of Christ. If only we could read this book carefully and listen attentively we would find the answers to all of our life's questions. Jesus is the Word of God and the light of the world, the light that brings light to those in darkness. Jesus reveals to us God's hidden presence, the God who says, "I am with you," the God who is the beauty of our world and the grace of our nature. Jesus makes God's presence known to us because Jesus *is* God's presence to us, the God enfleshed in human skin with a human face, the God who is closer to each of us than we can imagine.

I often look to Francis of Assisi to learn how to read the Book of Life. I must admit that most saints can help us here but Francis was particularly attentive to this book and so he is a good example for us. As we said before, Francis did not start out in life particularly religious. However, he had a profound experience of God and this seemed to touch him deeply enough that he began to change the habits of his life in order to pursue the gospel. Francis spent long hours in solitary prayer. Bonaventure says that he devoted himself entirely to prayer. Long hours of prayer seem to be essential to reading the Book of Life. Our Western culture is so fast moving and fragmented that spending more than an hour doing anything is entirely too long. Even medications are formulated now to work quickly and effectively so we can move on with our active lives. But Francis would spend days, weeks and months at prayer, usually in a small hermitage atop a mountain. He had a good memory and his biographers tell us that when he heard the gospel read (since he himself had a limited ability to read), he would commit to memory those passages that particularly impressed him. Reading the Book of Life, for Francis, was more than reading a text, it was instead reading the lines of our poor fragile human nature as shown to us in the poor and humble Christ.

In some way "reading" the Book of Life for Francis was similar to what the monks practiced: *lectio divina*—slow meditation on the words of Scripture, "chewing and digesting" them to make them one's own, and allowing these words to lead one into deeper relationship with God. Francis committed to memory the words of Scripture, incorporated them into his own daily life, and allowed himself to be transformed by them. Thomas of Celano wrote:

> The brothers who lived with him know
> that daily, constantly, talk of Jesus was always on his lips
>
> . . .

He was always with Jesus:
Jesus in his heart,
Jesus in his mouth,
Jesus in his ears,
Jesus in his eyes,
Jesus in his hands,
he bore Jesus always in his whole body.

. . .

Often as he walked along a road,
thinking and singing of Jesus,
he would forget his destination
and start inviting all the elements
to praise Jesus.[11]

Reading the Book of Life gave Francis new meaning to the world around him. He began to read the Book of Life in the book of the world because the Book of Life gave him "insight"—new vision. He read the Book of Life in lepers and poor people because he saw in them the goodness of God. "In all the poor," Bonaventure wrote, "that most Christian poor man [Francis] also saw before him / a portrait of Christ."[12] He read the Book of Life in birds, flowers and all other living creatures. He realized that he was related to each of them as "brother" because each had their source in the goodness of God and reflected that goodness in their own particular and unique way. In the Book of Life Francis also realized his own limitations, his fragility and sinfulness, and it was in knowing how fragile he really was that he became a great lover of God. The Book of Life gave Francis a new self-knowledge and this knowledge liberated him from a false self. Reading the Book of Life gave Francis great insight to the poverty of being human, that is, being radically dependent on God. "What a person is before God," he said, "that he is and no more."[13] When we read the Book of Life we recognize our human poverty, which makes us free to be with God and for God. The Book of Life liberated Francis to throw himself into the infinite embrace of God's love. When we live in God and God lives in us then we see the world for what it truly is—pregnant with God.

In the Book of Life we discover that all of creation tells us something about God—his power, wisdom and goodness. Stars, leaves, ladybugs, trees, flowers and humans, all in some way, bespeak God. Humans, of course, reflect God in the most explicit way because we are made in the image of God and thus have a capacity of likeness to God. But if we consider that every living element of creation, from quarks and leptons to atoms and humans, express the Word of God, then we might say that Incarnation has been happening for a very long time, indeed, ever since God uttered the eternal "yes" to a finite lover. All of creation is incarnational. That is why when Jesus, the Word made flesh, came among us, there was a "perfect fit" because all along creation was prepared to receive the fullness of the Word into it. As Bonaventure reminds us, Christ is not ordained to us but rather we are ordained to Christ.[14] Christ is the noble perfection of creation. Scotus would say Jesus Christ is the blueprint for creation because Christ is first in God's intention to love.[15] To think that from the very "beginning" (whatever that beginning may be) Christ and creation were destined to be co-lovers of God! This idea gives us quite a different image of God than one who is judge and king and who sent the Son because of corrupted human nature.

You might wonder why I am speaking about Jesus Christ to you in this way. I suppose one reason is that I am trying to explain the mystery of God's presence to you as well as myself. Jesus was not just a nice man who lived in Palestine. Perhaps I said this before but sometimes I get the impression that we think of Jesus as a really good person who did good deeds and nothing more. It seems to me that many people do not see the relation between Jesus and God (and even less so, between Jesus and the Trinity), as if these might be two separate realities that really have nothing in common. What I am trying to say here is simply that the mystery of God is a single mystery and Jesus, the Word of God, is the heart of that mystery. Bonaventure puts the parts of the mystery together in a harmonious whole. That is why I often look to him to explain the mystery of God. Bonaventure realized that we are created through the eternal Word and return to God through the incarnate Word, so the Word is central to our relationship with God.

And because the humility of God has been made known to us through the Word made flesh we are able to know the meaning of our lives, as well as the meaning of all created reality in and through Jesus. The humility of God means that God is hidden in Jesus and yet revealed in his actions of love, especially his love unto death on the cross. From his poor humble birth, throughout his life, to his death on the cross, Jesus is the clue to the whole universe. In Christ God bends low to embrace us (and all creation) in love. Christ is the key to our relationship with God, and God's relationship with us. As Bonaventure and Scotus remind us, all of creation is made for Christ and will not rest until it rests in Christ. The entire universe is "Christic."

If we understand the Incarnation as God bending low in love, we will understand God's presence in our lives and in our world. No longer will we ask "where is God?" or "how does God act?" We will know the answer in this simple statement: "God humbly and lovingly bends low to embrace us." In fact, God bends so low that we do not recognize his presence. God is so close to that which he embraces that he becomes one with it while never being anything less than God. Incarnation is about God's *involved goodness* in creation. It is because God is so eternally diffusive in love that God can give himself completely to us and lose nothing in the self-gift. So if we think Jesus is merely a good man we are entirely mistaken. Jesus is the Word of God through whom all things are made and all things find their completion. We must continue to read this Book of Life and dwell on it if we want to know the meaning of our lives, why we are here and where we are going.

There is a further point of interest that is worth noting. Bonaventure, like Scotus, did not view the Incarnation primarily as an event due to sin. This view, of course, is not to deny sin. Driving to work in the morning will affirm the reality of sin for most people. But sin is not the primary reason for Christ and our lives in Christ. Although Bonaventure was aware of the brokenness of the world (after all, he was Minister General in very turbulent times), he described the Incarnation as the completion of the created order. In Bonaventure's view, sin is real but love heals and makes whole. What if we were to think of human nature not as *fallen* nature, but as *incomplete* nature? Instead of sin being a tragic fall over the precipice of God's relationship to us, sin is every-thing that stands in the way of our completion in God.[16] As Zachary Hayes writes: "Sin is not a mere infringement of a law extrinsic to our nature. It is a failure to realize the potentiality of our nature itself. It is the resistance to expansion through union with others."[17] Similarly, what if we consider Christ not as a Savior from sin but as the One who heals us and makes us whole by an outpouring of God's love and mercy, the One who calls us to universal community? That is, what if we really believed that from all eternity Christ was destined to come as the per-fect lover of God and we were destined to be co-lovers in Christ? As Bonaventure indicates, Christ completes the order of creation but *we* complete the work of Christ. The world is made by God but brought to fullness of relationship with God by us humans because of our "perfect fit" to the Word of God.

This compatibility between Christ and us is not a custom-tailored fit for *Christians* alone. Rather, from the beginning of creation God made it possible for *all* of created nature to receive the Word into it; we and the cosmos are joined together. The whole evolutionary time of cre-ation has been a time of preparation to receive the fullness of the Word. When the Word became flesh, Bonaventure writes, the end was joined with the beginning, the first with the last, God with human, and the completion of the created order was realized.[18] Yet, it is not entirely complete. Take a look around. Does this world look complete to you? If this is what completion looks like, with wars, violence, earthquakes and other disasters abounding, what does incompletion look like? So Christ completes the order of creation but it is still incomplete. How do we make sense of this?

The Franciscan tradition maintains that Christ is the primary lover of the infinite love of God—the whole reason for creation is Christ. Jesus, we might say, is the "big bang" of the human potential for God because in his unique person, he realized the created capacity for God. As the Christ, the Anointed One of God, Jesus is God-with-us, the human One who mediates our relationship with God for all eternity. What happened in Jesus, however, must take place in all humanity (and creation) in order for the fullness of Christ to be realized, that is, in order for transformation of all created reality in God to be fulfilled. We might say that Jesus is the Christ but Christ is more than Jesus because Christ is all of humanity and creation as we are intended to be in the risen One, Jesus the Word incarnate, who is our permanent openness to the mystery of God's infinite love.

Bonaventure reflected on the completion of all things in Christ and suggested that the fullness of Christ depends on us because we are made in the image of Christ, the Word incarnate who is the true image of the Father.[19] The mystery of Christ and our human lives are intertwined. Because we humans complete the fullness of Christ by our participation in the Christ mystery, we are called to be co-creators of the universe, to "christify" the universe by our actions of love.[20] We are, as we said before, "little words" of the Word of God. So when all the little words of creation (us humans) come to the truth of our identity in Christ, when we allow God's image to shine forth in us, then the mystery of Christ grows because God becomes enfleshed in us—until eventually God becomes all in all. We are called to "put on Christ," so that the God who bends low in love bends low not in the historical person of Jesus alone but in Jesus risen—the Christ—in you and me in whom Jesus lives. God is humbly present among us because God is intimately present in you and me.

The problem is that while God never fails in bending low in love, we, in our fragmented, incomplete natures are often turned away from God. Sin, in Bonaventure's view, entails a turning from the good and a turning toward nothingness because without God, the self is "no-thing" in itself.[21] With sin we are bent over, blinded in intellect, distorted in will and entangled in endless questions. "The human person is endlessly asking and begging," Bonaventure writes. "Covetousness is never satisfied."[22] So while God is bent down in love for us we are bent over in love for ourselves, caught in a web of self-centeredness, to the extent that we fail to grasp the hand of God; we fail to see the humility of God. To live in relation to a humble God we must stand upright in order to know truth, to love rightly, and to act justly. "This occurs," Bonaventure says, "when someone turns completely away from self and toward God."[23]

While the grace of God is with us to help us turn in the right direction, God's grace is marked by freedom. God will not force us to love him, to stand upright. We must say "yes" to God. The grace of God that empowers us to say "yes" is always with us but still we must choose to say "yes." Freedom is one of the most difficult gifts God has given to creation. Freedom means choice and it corresponds to the fact that we are contingent beings, finite and changeable, radically dependent on God. Freedom, according to the handbook of modern culture, means radical independence, autonomy, the attitude of "nobody can tell me what to do" or "it's my life, I will do as I please." Such freedom, however, is not really freedom at all—it is enslavement to a radically self-centered ego and it makes one independent and isolated. After a certain amount of cultural freedom, one wonders why he or she exists at all. Suicide sometimes follows. Cultural freedom can be deadly.

True freedom is rooted in God. We come from a Trinity of love, we are immersed in a Trinity of love, and we are destined to share in this Trinity of love. We are by nature relational beings. Freedom does not mean to be free *from* relationships. Rather, it means to be free *for* relationships. Ultimately, it is relationship with God that gives us the greatest freedom to be the best of what we are created to be. I think that is why the natural world is always replete with beauty because the relationship between God and living things is simple. Flowers do not have a radically self-centered ego, so they are more naturally oriented toward the goodness of God. Trees do not choose to isolate themselves from leaves, birds, squirrels and other living creatures. Trees accept God's involved goodness and, as such, radiate a certain beauty. Humans, on the other hand—those who are created in the image of God—have free will and can make free choices, choices that either blur the image of God or sometimes make it so ugly that it is unrecognizable. True freedom is what makes us beautiful in God because we can be fully ourselves without having to make excuses for our weaknesses.

Human freedom is grounded in divine freedom. We are free because we are born out of the love of God and love is free. Perfect love is perfectly free. The Fathers of the church recognized that God becomes *powerless* before human freedom; he cannot violate it since it flows from his own omnipotence. Simply put, God creates human freedom and therefore he cannot violate what he creates. The orthodox theologian Vladimir Lossky writes:

> Certainly man was created by the will of God alone; but he cannot be deified by it alone. A single will for creation, but two for deification. A single will to raise up the image, but two to make the image into a likeness. The love of God for man is so great that it cannot constrain; for there is no love without respect. Divine will always will submit itself to gropings, to detours, even to revolts of human will to bring it to a free consent....God [is] a beggar of love waiting at the soul's door without ever daring to force it.[24]

This is a powerful statement that speaks to us of God's powerful love. The powerfulness of God, however, is a paradox; it is perceived as powerlessness in the divine risk of creation. The human person is the highest creation of God only because God gives it the possibility of love, and therefore of refusal. God risks the eternal ruin of his highest creation, precisely that it may be the highest.

Oftentimes, we confuse freedom with contingency. Contingency means that things can be otherwise—you may be alive today but you may be dead tomorrow. Freedom means the ability to live the fullness of life, an inward liberation from the chains of the mind and heart that weigh us down. It means being able to love someone more than one's own life, for the sake of the other. I once heard of a woman in prison who became so deeply contemplative in prayer that when the time of her release came, she did not want to leave. She had found God in the walls of a prison and in that discovery she had become free. Francis of Assisi also was a free man. Poverty emancipated Francis from the need to possess so that he could be free for God, free to follow the footprints of Jesus and to accept suffering as a way of uniting with Jesus on the cross. "As followers of most holy poverty," Celano wrote, "since they had nothing, they loved nothing; so they feared losing nothing."[25] Francis and his early followers remind us that it is not place or circumstances that make us free; it is the heart that makes us free when it is turned toward God. Bonaventure once wrote: "You truly exist where you love not merely where you live."[26] It is love that makes us free. And where you truly love, you are free.

Freedom is the gift of God's humble love. It is the gift of a God who loves us faithfully despite our failures, always bending low to embrace us in love. God's love is free because real love always desires the best for the other without interfering or manipulating the other. God is one who neither manipulates nor interferes with our created freedom. Rather, God respects the gift of freedom that he has given us. If God forced us to love him, God would not be perfect love and we would not be free. We would be puppets of a controlling God, a God who would be like a dictator; we would live under constant oppression. This would not be a God faithful in love and worthy of our trust and hope. But God does not control or manipulate. No, God is like a beggar waiting at the soul's door. If we choose to open the door and allow God into our lives, then we will find the freedom of love to be all that we are created to be.

Jesus was a free man because he was rooted in love and compassion. He was free to heal lepers and sinners, to let women touch and kiss him; he was free to speak the truth against injustice, to turn over tables in the temple, to speak about God's reign with authority. Jesus was free because he was rooted in the love of God and, therefore, humble. Ultimately, Jesus was free enough to offer his life as a sacrifice for the sake of God's truth. Humbly rooted in love, Jesus was free to die on a cross. And in that freedom, God's freedom of love was revealed, the love that brings about a new future. The cross signifies to us that if we are free enough to love then we are free enough to die, and if we are free to die then we are free to live. As long as we are in relation to a God who is freedom-in-love, then death will be part of our journey. For every distance of separation from God must be overcome by death, by giving up isolated existence for a greater union. Finite human life longs for fulfillment of relationship, for union, and only death can remove the veil that separates us from the infinite love of God. Yes, freedom is the gift of love but love prevails in freedom. Violence, suffering and death do not have the last word in God. The last word is love. That is why those who follow Christ, the saints, like Francis, are often dangerous because they are free. No harm can be done to them because they have already died into God. "Blessed are those whom death will find in Your most holy will," Francis wrote, "for *the second death* shall do them no harm."[27] To be free is to be able to live in truth, to love radically and to act justly by living the grace of costly discipleship. Freedom in God is what makes Christ alive in our world. We are called to be humble and free in love, like Jesus, that we may help move the world toward unity in love.

REFLECTION QUESTIONS

1. What is your understanding of Jesus Christ at the present time? Do you read the "Book of Life" to find meaning and insight into your own life?

2. How do you understand the relationship between God and Christ at the present? How do you relate the humility of God to your own following of Christ?

3. What are some ways you can deepen your life in the humility of God? How can this understanding change your life as a Christian in the world?

NOTES

[1] For a discussion on this topic see Ilia Delio, "Revisiting the Franciscan Doctrine of Christ," *Theological Studies* 64 (2003): 3–23.

[2] Zachary Hayes, "Christ, Word of God and Exemplar of Humanity," 6.

[3] Hayes, Christ, Word of God and Exemplar of Humanity," *Cord* 46.1 (1996): 7.

[4] William Short, *The Franciscans* (Wilmington, Del.: Michael Glazier,1989), p. 115.

[5] This is how Bonaventure begins his "Sermon II on the Nativity of the Lord." See *What Manner of Man?*, p. 57.

[6] Bonaventure, *Lig.vit.* 26 (VIII, 78). Cousins, trans. *Bonaventure*, p. 149.

[7] Hayes, commentary on "Sermon II on the Nativity of the Lord," pp. 89–90, n. 41.

[8] Hayes, commentary on "Sermon II," pp. 89–90, n. 41.

[9] Bonaventure, "The Major Legend of Saint Francis," 9.1. Cousins, trans. *Bonaventure*, p. 263.

[10] "The Remembrance of the Desire of a Soul by Thomas of Celano," 124 in *FA:ED* II, pp. 353–354.

[11] "The Life of Saint Francis by Thomas of Celano," 9 in *FA:ED* I, pp. 283–284.

[12] Bonaventure, "The Major Legend of Saint Francis," 8.5 in *FA:ED* II, p. 589.

[13] Bonaventure, "The Major Legend of Saint Francis," 6.1 in *FA:ED* II, p. 569.

[14] Bonaventure, III *Sent*. d. 32, q. 5, ad 3 (III, 706). *"Non enim Christus ad nos finaliter ordinatur, sed nos finaliter ordinamur ad ipsum."*

[15] The Franciscan scholar Bill Short in an unpublished lecture, states that Scotus's writings help us to see that "before anything is poured out as creation, what God is expressing is what this body of Christ is....This means that, in the first chapter of Genesis, sun, moon, trees, animals, stones, all have life only in Christ, through Christ, and with Christ, for 'in the beginning was the Word' (John 1:1). All in the material bodily world are Christological and express what the body of Christ is like. Everything out there—trees, clouds, all—is formed to give us part of the picture of who Christ is in the Incarnation, the concreteness of God." Cited in Margaret Pirkl, "Christ, The Inspiration and Center of Life with God and Creation," in *Resource Manual for the Study of Franciscan Christology*, Kathleen Moffatt and Christa Marie Thompson, eds. (Washington, D.C.: Franciscan Federation, 1998), p. 264.

[16] This is Bonaventure's redemption-completion theory of salvation, which Zachary Hayes discusses in his book *The Hidden Center: Spirituality and Speculative Christology in St. Bonaventure* (New York: The Franciscan Institute, 1981), pp. 155–191.

[17] Zachary Hayes, *A Window to the Divine: A Study of Christian Creation Theology* (Quincy, Ill.: Franciscan Press, 1997), p. 93.

[18] See Bonaventure's "Sermon II on the Nativity of the Lord," in *What Manner of Man?*, pp. 57–75.

[19] Bonaventure is not the first in the Christian tradition to ponder the idea that the fullness of Christ lies in creation. In the twelfth century the Cistercian monk Isaac of Stella argued that our salvation is necessary for the "completion" of Christ. See Caroline Walker Bynum, *Jesus as Mother: Studies in the Spirituality of the High Middle Ages* (Berkeley, Ca.: University of California Press, 1982), p. 95.

[20] The idea of the Christian vocation as "Christifying matter" was Teilhard's passion. Only in this way, he realized, can the new heaven and earth that we long for be attained. He also realized, however, that traditional theology prevents the Christian from being passionately involved in the world. See Christopher F. Mooney, "Teilhard de Chardin and Christian Spirituality," in *Process Theology*, pp. 308–315.

[21] Bonaventure, *Bonaventure: Mystic of God's Word* "Prologue to the Second Book of Sentences," Timothy Johnson, trans. (New York: New City Press, 1999), p. 62.

[22] Bonaventure, "Prologue to the Second Book of Sentences," p. 63.

[23] Bonaventure, "Prologue to the Second Book of Sentences," p. 60.

[24] Lossky, *Orthodox Theology*, p. 73.

[25] "The Life of Saint Francis by Thomas of Celano," 15.39 in *FA:ED* I, p. 218.

[26] Bonaventure, *Soliloquium* 2.12 (VIII, 49). Zachary Hayes, trans. *Bonaventure: Mystical Writings* (New York: Crossroad, 1999), p. 140. Bonaventure writes: "O my soul, I think that you exist more truly where you love than where you merely live, since you are transformed into the likeness of whatever you love, through the power of this love itself."

[27] Francis of Assisi, "The Canticle of the Creatures," 13 in *FA:ED* I, p.114.

Chapter Four

A GOD OF FAITHFUL LOVE

I have loved you with an everlasting love,
so I am constant in my affection for you.
—Jeremiah 31:3

We have been speaking up to now in the language of theology, trying to understand the profound mystery of God's humility through a Franciscan lens. Theology is "God-talk" but "God-talk" is not exactly "people-talk" and many of us find it dry, abstract, somewhat lofty and perhaps boring. Sometimes we want to cut through all the abstract language and get to the heart of the matter with our questions· What is God? Where is God? What is God doing in my life? What is God doing in this world that seems to be such a mess at times? But our answers would have no real content if we did not take the time to reflect on the mystery of God and God's relationship to us. And so we have entered into the inner world of the Trinity and the mystery of the Incarnation. Now, hopefully, we are ready to look more deeply at God's relationship to us.

There are many ways to explore this relationship but I, personally, have three main areas of interest and so it is these areas I will share with you over the next several chapters. The first area of interest is evolution. Evolution, according to the new science today, is what accounts for the development of life in the universe from both a biological and cosmological perspective. Scientists today tell us that life began with a bang—literally. Origen of Alexandria once described the beginning of creation as the clashing of symbols, as if the universe was a great symphony. However creation began, the universe gradually unfolded with its fabric of forces and fields until small isolated structures gave way to more complex unions and eventually to human beings.[1] I believe that evolution accounts not only for physical life but for spiritual life as well. In a universe centered in Christ, the evolution of the material world is a drive toward spirit. This is what I hope our discussion on the humility of God will ultimately lead us to appreciate, the evolution of Christian life in the universe.

My second area of concern is suffering and whether or not God suffers. To me this is an important question for our age, which has known violence and terrorism and still lingers in the aftermath of the horrible atrocities of the twentieth century. The question of *theodicy*, or why God allows evil (especially a God of love), is a question that continuously filters through films, books and various media. Is God involved in a world of suffering or is God immune to human suffering? There are no immediate answers to the difficult questions of suffering but I hope that we can come to a better insight of God's relationship to a world of suffering through an understanding of God's humble love.

Finally, I will take up the question of pluralism and difference. We live in an age of "global spirituality;" at least that is the latest buzzword. But what does global spirituality mean in light of Christian spirituality? For some, it means that Christ is an obstacle to world unity and therefore we must move toward a post-Christian age. For others, the idea of global spirituality provides a warm, fuzzy feeling that we are all somehow united even though, when we get beneath the surface of things, few people want to sacrifice their comfortable lives for a stranger. Globalism, however, is here to stay. For Christians, it is essential that we come to a deeper insight of Christ in a global world if our lives in Christ are to have any real meaning and contribute to the evolution of the world. Coming to understand the meaning of Christ in light of plurality and difference can help move Christians out of a theology of the Middle Ages and into the future.

In this chapter, I would like to discuss God's involvement in a physical world of change and complexity. For the past several years, I have been involved in the science and religion dialogue, working primarily on the question of how God acts in an evolutionary world. It is difficult to live with a humble God in a world of change. Oftentimes, we want God to act visibly in our lives, in a way that we could say, "now I know what I should do" or "I understand why that happened." We seek a God of power and might—one we can visibly detect in our lives. But science is changing our view of the world and this new view is changing our understanding of how God acts in the world.

As contemporary believers, we live between two worlds. In our everyday experience, we live in a culture deeply conditioned by the insights and theories of modern science, especially evolution and quantum physics. But in the context of the church, its theology and its liturgy, we live in a pre-modern world marked by a static, hierarchical universe. The church as a whole displays a perfect, firm, solid and irrefutable order. At the top stands Christ, our hierarch. Next, there is the pope who occupies the highest place in the hierarchy, and then come the bishops, clergy and finally the ordinary faithful.[2] So on one hand we live with rapid change, on the other hand we live with a static God and a fixed church. The problem is, these two worlds do not complement each other, and we often find ourselves falling between the cracks of separation asking "where is God in our everyday lives?"

We live in an ancient and evolutionary universe. It is not exactly the universe according to the story of creation found in Genesis, sketched out neatly in six days with a Sabbath on the seventh day. Rather, the universe as we know it originated in a fiery Big Bang some fifteen billion years ago.[3] It started extremely simple, an almost uniform expanding ball of energy, which exploded in a "big bang." What is fascinating is that immediately after the "bang" the universe started to cool at an incredibly precise rate such that all the forces of the universe formed in the first three minutes. Some scientists say that from its beginning, the universe was "fine-tuned" for the emergence of human life; or to take it a step further, one might assert that the human mind was built into the universe from the onset. Others say that it is simply coincidence that the elements in the universe were appropriate for the emergence of life—a stroke of cosmic luck. However we consider the unfolding of the universe, the fact is that after fifteen billion years of evolving history, the universe has become richly diverse and structured, with us humans at the growing tip of its expansion. After fifteen billion years, a tiny ball of energy has become the home of saints and sinners.

The mystery of a cosmic evolutionary world lies not simply in asking the question, "who lit the fire?" but rather in understanding that God creates slowly and continues to hold the world in being even after fifteen billion years![4] While the universe itself has been an evolving history, biological life on earth has had its own slow unfolding. Scientists tell us today that life on Earth originated about 3.8 billion years ago. It did not begin with bipedal hominids but with bacteria and single-celled organisms. The slow emergence of life, especially human life, raises questions as to how God acts in the world if, indeed, God "acts" at all. Charles Darwin, in his classic *On the Origin of Species*, described the evolution of biological life according to mechanisms found within nature: natural selection, adaptation and survival of the fittest. The contemporary theologian John Haught, states that "because chance, blind selection, and enormously 'wasteful' periods of time are so ingredient to the unfolding of life, Darwin's picture of nature would appear to raise difficulties about the idea of God."[5] While Darwin accounted for the appearance of life according to mechanisms "built into" nature, William Paley writes of intelligent design in nature. Paley imagines that if we were to walk across a patch of ground and stumble upon a watch and opened it up to view its intricate parts, we would conclude that it was the product of intelligent design. Similarly, we should be able to reason that the intricate order in the natural world points toward the world's creation by an intelligent designer. Paley's argument emphasizes God as the ultimate designer of life, an argument that continues to the present day. So while Darwin's theory gradually pushed God aside, Paley's argument has made a Creator God essential to the intricate order of creation.

In the seventeenth century the famous mathematician Sir Isaac Newton developed laws of motion that changed our view of the universe right up to the twentieth century. According to Newton, the world is governed according to rules and regulations; it is an ordered product or machine designed by a creator. Just as a clock has different parts put together by a clockmaker, so too, the world is designed by a God who created the world machine, set it in motion, retired among the stars and intervenes once in a while to fine-tune the machine. As the ultimate designer and Maker of the world machine, God, Newton believed, not only controls the machine but is responsible for its parts. The notion of the world as a totality of parts led to a "mechanistic" view of the world. When parts of the machine wore down or burnt out, they were to be replaced. The whole point of the world machine was continuous function. If something was wrong with the machine, one had only to check the parts. If the part was dysfunctional, it could be replaced and the machine could continue to work. We find this same mechanistic view in church and society today. Nations, communities, churches and families are all reducible to the individuals who constitute them. The institutional church tells us to obey God, keep the commandments, follow the rules and you will be on the right road to heaven. If sin is prevalent among the group (similar to a malfunctioning part) see to it that it is removed so the machine (the church or local community) can continue to function routinely. Barbara Brown Taylor states, "if you walk into many churches, you will hear God described as a being who behaves almost as predictably as Newton's universe."[6]

Newton was a theist but other scientists believed that science itself would ultimately provide all the answers to the mystery of the world order. When asked about the place of God in his system Simon de La Place responded "we no longer have any need for such a hypothesis."[7] Those scientists who held to the "God hypothesis" sometimes used "God" to provide a reason to explain events when science could not provide answers. The use of God to explain events became known as the "God of the gaps" and is still in vogue today. When we ask "why did this happen?" and can provide no reasonable answer we say, "God did it." Or when we ask "what will happen tomorrow?" and want an answer we say, "God only knows." The name of God fills in the gaps when events cannot be reasonably explained. God can arrange for nice weather, create new jobs and prevent accidents. God intervenes in nature in unexplainable ways but without violating the laws of nature. God is the master designer of the universe. One wonders, however, in light of this idea, why God took fifteen billion years to develop human life at the cost of suffering and death. If God is in such control why do bad things happen to good people? Does God play favorites?

While the new science has not entirely dispensed with the laws of physics, we know that the universe is much different than what Newton described. The mechanistic view of the world associated with Newtonian physics has been replaced with a dynamic, open-ended view of the world in which some events are in principle unpredictable. At the infinitesimal level of the atom and its subatomic particles, quantum mechanics has uncovered a realm where time, space and matter itself behave according to laws whose very functioning have uncertainty built into them. While statistical probability lends a measure of order to this realm, precise subatomic events do not seem to occur according to any discernible regularity. The German physicist Werner Heisenberg formulated the "uncertainty principle" which asserts that a human observer cannot simultaneously plot both the position and velocity of a subatomic particle, for by charting one we disturb the other.[8] This principle has led to real debate as to whether or not there is real ontological indeterminacy in nature. Albert Einstein did not accept this theory, saying that God does not "play dice" with the universe. The idea of indeterminacy in nature certainly raises the question of God's action in the world. Does God control the outcome of events or not? Does God play dice? Many scientists agree that if there is chance in nature, it has its own laws and regulations. While the role of chance may enable matter to explore its potentialities, chance does not prevail over law nor is it an alternative to law. Rather, chance may be the means by which law is creative.[9]

Quantum physics has not only given us a new view of matter today as indeterminate but also as relational. The universe seems to be inherently relational. Newtonian physics pictured the collisions of individual atoms as taking place within the container of absolute space and in the course of the unfolding of an absolute time. Einstein's discovery of special relativity showed that the observers' judgments of spatial and temporal characters are relative to their states of motion. His description of general relativity integrated space, time and matter into a single unified account. Einstein showed that the geometry of the universe depends upon the disposition of matter within it, and the shape of that geometry will curve the paths along which the matter moves.[10] In a famous experiment with Boris Podolsky and Nathan Rosen, Einstein showed that once two entities have interacted with each other they remain mutually entangled however far they may eventually separate. If the particles are separated and one particle is placed on the moon and the other on someone's head, the spin of one particle in a positive direction will cause a complementary spin of the other particle in the opposite direction. Even though the particles are widely separated, they remain mutually related.

One of the most interesting scientific theories to emerge in the twentieth century is chaos theory. Scientists tell us today that one of the most astounding features of physical, biological and chemical systems is that they are open to change. Whereas in the Newtonian world physical reality was assumed to follow rigid causal pathways, today physical reality is seen to be open and "flexible" with the capacity not only to sustain change but to sustain novelty and spontaneity with an openness to future possibilities. Chaos is a word that the average person hardly associates with order and, yet, the science of chaos is primarily concerned with order.

Chaos theory is the study of "dynamical systems" in which complex and random behavior arises spontaneously out of simple and ordered physical processes. Changes occur within systems that cannot be ascribed to any one part. One of the most characteristic features of open systems is their sensitive dependency on initial conditions. Changes in initial conditions may give rise to new patterns of order. Since these spontaneous changes can emerge in systems under that guise of "disorder" the name "chaos" is attached. However, "chaos" is really order masquerading as randomness in systems.

The strange attractor is a basin of attraction within the system (but different from the system) that describes the shape of chaos or spontaneous movements of a system that deviate from the normal pattern of order. Since the strange attractor pulls the system into a visible shape, it ultimately causes a new pattern of order to emerge within the system. Some scientists have claimed that the appearance of the strange attractor means that order is inherent in chaos since the "attractor" itself is a novel pattern of order that arises spontaneously within a system. When systems are dislodged from a stable state, there is first a period of oscillation prior to a state of full chaos or a period of total unpredictability. It is during this time that the strange attractor seems to "spontaneously" appear. Very slight variations, so small as to be indiscernible, can amplify into unpredictable results when they are fed back on themselves.[11] These slight variations over time can have explosive results, resulting in surprising new patterns of order. The novelty of chaotic systems, therefore, is that fluctuations, randomness and unpredictability at the local level, in the presence of a strange attractor, cohere over time into definite and predictable forms. The system is pulled into new patterns of behavior. While many scientists maintain that there is a level of determinism in chaos (using non-linear equations) still chaos theory tells us that the world does not function according to law and certainty but according to chance and randomness. In this respect, chaos theory boggles the Western mind with its penchant for certainty, predictive power and control. Other societies are more willing to accept flux and uncertainty and to live within the flow of things. But chaos theory tells us that acceptance of a degree of uncertainty is essential to being alive in the universe. Complete knowledge and control will always elude us. In this respect I agree with John Haught who writes "a theology obsessed with order and design is ill-prepared for evolution."[12] Rather, as Haught asks, "what kind of universe should be ours if it is grounded in an infinitely compassionate Mystery that pours itself out into the world in unrestrained and vulnerable love?"[13]

When we think of creation, we may think of God as the grand designer of a large assembly plant called "human life." God makes things in a way that is quite mysterious to us but somehow we imagine God to be busy at work putting parts together to create plants, trees, crawling creatures, other types of creatures and human beings. But what if we were to imagine something different? What if we were to imagine that God doesn't really "do" things for us? What if God simply loves us, but loves us in such a perfect and absolute way that God can never desire anything else of us than our ultimate good? And ~~God loves us so perfectly and absolutely not because of what we do or what we are but because the Father perfectly and absolutely loves the Son~~. What I am suggesting to you is that perhaps the way God does things for us, or rather, the way God "acts," is really God's love for us, the love of the Father for the Son in the Spirit. I wonder what our world would be like if we lived in it as part of the Trinity's dance of love rather than as an object of design and control? We are simply unaware just how deeply immersed we are in the overflowing goodness of God.

The evolution of life in the universe tells us that our image of God as order-maker, planner and designer needs to change. This is a God of self-emptying love, a God of humble love, who takes all the time in the world to create, a God who invites rather than forces the world to realize new possibilities of being. This is not a God of the past but a God of the future. As John Haught writes

> in the crucified man Jesus—and not in philosophical rea-
> soning alone—Christian faith is given the key to God's
> relation to the world. The cross reveals the paradoxical
> closeness of the self absenting God from whose limitless
> generosity the world is called, but never forced, into being
> and becoming. God's power (the capacity to influence the
> world) is paradoxically made manifest in the vulnerable
> defenselessness of a crucified man.[14]

The revelation of divine power in the form of divine humility means that the universe is the outflow of infinite love, a love that does not manipulate or dissolve the beloved cosmos. Intrinsic to this notion of divine love, Haught states, is making a creation genuinely independent of its creator. Love does not compel or overwhelm. Rather, God leaves room in nature for randomness or accident. Even Thomas Aquinas realized that a world so rigidly controlled by God as to be devoid of accidents is theologically inconceivable. God is not a control-operator or a manipulator. God is love, a love that is dynamic, self-giving and free, a love that restrains itself in order to give the world space and time in which to become something distinct from the creative love that constitutes it as "other," a love that lets the other be.

It is in this respect we must consider the humility of God's love in the "act" of creation, in the whole unfolding of an evolutionary universe. What if we did not think of the cosmos as a unified whole but as a still-unfinished labor of creation? What if God does not control every event by might and power but allows creation its freedom to play while remaining faithful in love? What if God allows all the time in the world for the mystery of Christ to unfold, the mystery which is not of the past but of the future, that which is coming to be? To understand the mystery of Christ as the one who is "coming to be" is to come to a new understanding of how God "acts" in the universe. God does not act apart from Christ but with a view toward Christ. And if Christ is the litmus test of how God acts in the universe then we must confess that God acts according to love, mercy and compassion rather than design, control and intelligence. God acts according to what God is, a Trinity of persons united in humble love.

The notion of God's action as humble love is receiving new attention today. The German Lutheran theologian Jürgen Moltmann states that the logic of creation is the logic of love. "Creation is not a demonstration of God's boundless power," he writes, "it is the communication of God's love which knows neither premises nor preconditions."[15] Moltmann claims that God's creative activity outwards is preceded by a humble divine self-limitation, which does not simply begin with creation but, according to Moltmann, is grounded in God's self-humiliating love.[16] God makes a space within himself in order for creation to come into being. According to Moltmann, God creates a world that is not divine and preserves it by distancing himself from it. Divine omnipotence, therefore, is expressed as self-limitation or divine self-contraction. Similarly, John Haught states that God freely undergoes self-emptying (kenosis) so that something other than divine reality can come into existence. It is out of God's humility and loving concern for the integrity of the "other" that the universe is endowed, from its conception, with an inherent capacity for self-organization.[17] If the natural world has the capacity to self-organize, to regulate itself and to evolve into new forms of life then it does seem to be a world endowed with unlimited freedom. Does God take a risk in giving creation its own autonomy and independence?

Bonaventure offers a completely integral relationship between God and creation precisely because God is Trinity and the Word is center. The fecundity of God's inner life, the nature of which involves free self-communication, is the same fecundity that provides for the diversity of creation. The humility of God's love in creation is related to the fact that God is an infinite source of love. God is eternally fecund and self-communicative. As a coincidence of opposites, God's transcendent fecundity *is* God's immanence as self-giving love. This means that God can be fully involved in creation as self-communicative love while remaining transcendent in love. As Bonaventure writes, "creation is no more than a center or point compared to the immensity of God's goodness."[18] Here we might say that the input of energy into the space-time continuum that brings about change (creation) is none other than the love between the Father and Son. God does what God is—love. The fundamental relationship of the Father-Son/Word means that there is really only one primordial relationship (namely, the Father-Son-Spirit) both within the Trinity and in creation.[19] While creation flows out of the relationship between the Father and Son, the Father's goodness is really communicated to only one other, namely, the Son or Word who, as Word, expresses the Father's divine ideas.[20] The Father, by loving the Word, loves all things in and through the Word.[21] Since this relationship is the basis for all that exists, I have suggested that creation is an act of the Father's love for the Son and the mutuality of love united in the Spirit.[22] Since God's being is God's action and God's being is love, God's action is an eternal-temporal act of love.[23] Creation, as Denis Edwards notes, takes place and flourishes within the divine life.[24]

The idea of creation as a single eternal-temporal act of love is not entirely a new one. The Swiss theologian Hans Urs Von Balthasar described God's action in creation as "the play within the play."[25] That is, the drama of divine action in creation takes place within the drama of Trinitarian life. If we were to imagine this drama in the form of concentric circles we—humans and creation—would be the little circle contained within the larger circle of the Trinity; thus, the "play within a play." The drama for Balthasar is the drama of the Father's love, which is poured out—emptied—in the generation of the Son. This drama, he claims, surpasses all possible drama between a God and a world. He goes on to say that any world only has its place within the drama of the Father's love for the Son by which the distinction between the Father and Son is bridged by the Holy Spirit. Balthasar writes: "It is the drama of the 'emptying' of the Father's heart, in the generation of the Son, that contains and surpasses all possible drama between a God and a world. For any world only has its place within that distinction between Father and Son that is maintained and bridged by the Holy Spirit."[26] As Edwards states, "for Von Balthasar, every drama that can be played out in creation is already contained in and surpassed in the eternal 'event' of inner Trinitarian love whereby the Father begets the Word. The begetting of the Word is an eternal act of letting go, of divine *kenosis*, of creating space for the other."[27] If this becoming of the world is grounded in the eternal Trinitarian process, then it is reasonable to suggest, as Edwards does, "that God does not create discrete individual beings through a series of interventions, but rather God creates in one divine act that embraces the whole process. It is this one divine act that enables what is radically new to emerge in creation."[28] So even though we may think life on earth is full of drama, Balthasar tells us, every drama here is already contained in and surpassed in the eternal drama of inner Trinitarian love.

The drama of life is something of a stage show—lights, sound, color, action (lots of action), dance, music, laughter and tears. There is little drama in a single-cell amoeba. But life brews with questions of meaning and purpose when a baby is born, a parent dies, a friend is stricken with illness or a brother is lost in war. What Balthasar is saying is that the drama of these events is caught up in the drama of the Father's love for the Son united in the Spirit. If the drama of human life is marked by birth and death, by giving up and letting go for the sake of new life, then we might say that sacrifice or giving up for a greater good marks the drama of human life. Perhaps, as Jürgen Moltmann suggests, the cross exists from all eternity in the heart of God, in the self-emptying love of the Father for the Son.[29] Jesus, the image of the Father, reflects all of the Father's love to us, especially in the cross, where love is poured out for the healing of the world. What this means on a deeper level is that compassion is part of God's humility. Compassion is not an admirable trait that God acquired once he decided to have a creation. No, compassion is God's love that so extends itself to the other without asking for anything in return, that it may be one with the other in all things. The compassion of God is the Father stretching forth in love to the Son so that the Father is completely one in love with the Son. God is no stranger to the demands of love.

The idea that divine action is really one eternal-temporal act of love between the Father and Son is supported by the idea that the Trinity is a communion of persons-in-love. God is not an actor vis-à-vis the act of creation, as we find with models of divine action in which God is described as "efficient cause," a God who "does things" such as parting waters, sending locusts or puting the parts of a cell together.[30] Rather, as Bonaventure notes, God does not need to create since infinite fecundity lies within the Godhead itself. That God creates, however, reflects who God is, namely, self-communicative love. Because the nature of God lies precisely in fecundity, the question of "how" God creates cannot be separated from the question of "why" God creates, since the very nature of the Trinity as self-communicative love is itself the basis of action. Bonaventure's theology allows us to say that the triune God does not act on discrete levels of creation, as if connecting things together nor does God act in every single discrete event as an individual "actor." God does not "act" to cause things to change; rather, things change because God is love and love is attractive. God is a relationship of love whose "action" in creation is an eternal-temporal "act" of love. In light of this idea, I would suggest that instead of talking about creation as divine action, it may be more reasonable to talk about creation as divine relationship.[31] Just as the Father is related to the Son in and through the Spirit, so too, God is related to creation.

Martin Buber, in his book *I and Thou*, claimed that two human beings by their dynamic interrelation co-create what he called "the Between" (*das Zwischen*), a meeting place where the two subjectivities can influence and affect one another without danger of the one being absorbed into the other as an accidental modification of the other's existence and activity.[32] Applied to the God-world relationship, we can say that creation takes place *das Zwischen*, that is, precisely in the relationship between God and the object of God's love.[33] As the finite self-expression of God's fecund goodness, creation continues to exist because the Father loves the Son in the Spirit, that is, because God is love. Since God's love can never be fully exhausted by its very nature of being infinite, so too creation has no other goal than that of perfect goodness which is participation in the intense generosity of Being itself.

If divine action is the relationship between the Trinity and creation, we might say that the Trinity of love is always attracting creation as the beloved, as the Father attracts the Son in the eternal breath of the Spirit's love. It is in and through the Son as exemplar and the Spirit as life that the Father embraces creation. Creation is grounded in the primordial *mystery* of Trinitarian love. It is the attractive loving power of the Father-Son-Spirit relationship, which "creates" temporally (by the power of attraction) with a view toward love. Using the metaphor from chaos theory we may say that the triune God is a "strange attractor."[34] In and through the divine Word, the Trinity is present to creation as involved goodness, yet transcendent in divine fecundity.

As a strange attractor, God is always luring creation toward the more or, we might say, the optimal good. Since creation is replete with goodness, there are many possibilities in creation for the optimal good to be realized. God's desire for that which God creates means that creation cannot be in a state of equilibrium or at rest but rather is always dynamically oriented toward the triune God. Creation, therefore, is not radically separate from God; rather it is a *free* limited expression of the infinite goodness of God, although without exhausting the divine good, which is both immanently diffusive and infinitely transcendent. Since goodness and being are radically co-extensive, according to Bonaventure, being cannot remain autonomous and independent (self-contained) but must seek to share itself with another.

Being is dynamic, characterized by a spirit of energy that impels it to change.[35] Creation, therefore, is not only "expressed goodness" but, as the expression of divine goodness, it is dynamic and relational. It is always "becoming" since it is always in the process of stretching forth unto another.

For Bonaventure, God's humble love in creation by which God is turned toward creation is related to the fact that God is an infinite source of love. God is eternally fecund and self-communicative. As a coincidence of opposites, God's transcendent nature of absolute goodness *is* God's immanence as self-giving love. As he writes: "God's power is his humility; God's strength is his weakness; God's greatness is his lowliness."[36] This means that God who is infinitely transcendent is intimately present to creation but in a hidden way. The divine fecundity of self-diffusive goodness in creation is a limited expression of the infinite mystery of God who is love, although it is a limited expression of love that is freely shared. This provides a more congruent relationship between God and creation that does not suggest divine risk or vulnerability. Rather, God is absolute freedom in love. As freedom *in love* God's freedom is God's fidelity to the other, that is, to creation. As freedom in love God is turned toward creation in humility and is present to creation as humble self-giving love or ultimate goodness. This commitment is not one of necessity, but one of freedom. God allows the other to be precisely through the commitment of love. Moltmann writes: "God [therefore] does what for him is axiomatic— what is divine. In doing this he is entirely free, and in this freedom he is entirely himself."[37] John Haught notes, "even in human relations we are most responsive to others whose love takes the shape of a non-interference that gives us the slack to be ourselves. We feel most liberated, and most alive, in the presence of those who risk letting us be ourselves."[38] In short, love does not manipulate or control but rather seeks the best for the other. In Bonaventure's view, God commits himself to creation through fidelity in love by allowing creation to be itself.

The notion of an infinitely loving and humble God at work in the universe overturns the image of God as a tyrannical force who dictates the events of the universe. Creation is not the amusement of a lonely deity. Rather God's power is the fidelity of God's humble love that allows creation to follow its own internal laws and designs. Divine omnipotence is the divine capacity for love beyond all human comprehension, as Walter Kasper writes. "It requires omnipotence to be able to surrender oneself and give oneself away; and it requires omnipotence to be able to take oneself back in the giving and to preserve the independence and freedom of the recipient. Only an almighty love can give itself wholly to the other and be a helpless love."[39] God's power is not coercive "power over" but it is sovereign love which empowers. God does not control the universe; rather, God is related to it as humble love and thus remains constantly faithful in love. The notion that the *humble* love of God comprises the inner force of the created universe underscores the notion of a *self-organizing* universe, one that can entertain chance, randomness and complexity, and give rise to beauty and order that can be intelligibly perceived. This divine self-restraining character is fully compatible with God's love which, rather than being rigidly deterministic, is total self-giving in freedom and creativity for the sake of the good which both gives rise to created being and, essentially, is being. Whatever we say about God as creator, therefore, must correspond to the humility of God and to the nature of God as self-communicative love.

It is in light of God's humble love that we must abandon the pursuit of complete knowledge and control. These will always elude us. We are in relation to a God who hides in the ordinary events and things of the world, who allows creation to take chances, who enjoys new possibilities, in short, a God who doesn't mind the messiness of creation. As finite creatures, total knowledge and power will always be beyond us; thus, we would do well to learn to live comfortably with a certain measure of uncertainty, paradox and ambiguity. Francis of Assisi learned this lesson in life in his own simple way. He trusted God's infinite and involved goodness in creation. He somehow knew that God had endowed creation (including humans) with an abundance of possibilities and potentialities. Francis did not live a rigid life but celebrated the goodness of creation and the many possibilities within it. I will end with a story that indicates to us Francis' trust in God's humble love.

According to legend, Francis and brother Masseo were traveling in Tuscany when they came to a crossroad. Masseo asked which road they would take. Francis said they would take the road God wanted them to take, and Masseo asked how they would know. At this Francis commanded Masseo to twirl around until Francis told him to stop. Then, Francis asked which way he was facing. When Masseo answered, Francis said that was the way they would follow.[40] Did God preordain one direction in which Francis and Masseo were to go or did the direction arise simply by chance? Such a question probably did not occur to Francis for what he realized is that God is in every direction; the goodness of God has no limits. God who is humble in love is faithful in love. In the same way, creation may take its chances and display its disorder, and similarly we humans may live chaotically but in all things God's love prevails. Francis not only trusted in God's humble love but he moved within creation as if he were held safely within the Trinity of love. Perhaps if we live in the freedom of love and strive not for control but for acceptance and trust in God's faithfulness, as creation seems to, the world will move toward its goal, toward Christ, and this will be the unity of all things in love.

REFLECTION QUESTIONS

1. What are some of the ways you consider God "acting" in the world? In your life?
2. How do you understand Balthasar's idea that creation is a single act of the Trinity and we are caught up in this act as a "drama within the drama"? Does the idea of living within the drama of Trinitarian life change the way you trust in God? Hope in God? Relate to God?
3. How does the story of Francis and Masseo speak to you of God's action in your life? In creation?

NOTES

[1] Denis Edwards offers a succinct summary of the universe story in his book *Breath of Life: A Theology of the Creator Spirit* (Maryknoll, Orbis, 2004), pp. 7–15.

[2] This is Max Wildiers's description of the church in the Middle Ages but it still speaks to us today. See N. Max Wildiers, *The Theologian and His Universe: Theology and Cosmology from the Middle Ages to the Present*, Paul Dunphy, trans. (New York: Seabury Press, 1982), p. 73.

[3] The most recent estimate of the age of the universe is 14.7 billion years. See *Science & Theology News* (July/August 2004): 12.

[4] John Polkinghorne, "Physics and Metaphysics in a Trinitarian Perspective," *Theology and Science* 1.1 (2003): 39–40.

[5] John F. Haught, "Evolution and God's Humility: How Theology Can Embrace Darwin," *Commonweal* 127 (2000): 12.

[6] Barbara Brown Taylor, "Physics and Faith: The Luminous Web," *The Christian Century* (June 2-9, 2000): 613.

[7] Wildiers, *The Theologian and His Universe*, p. 101.

[8] Elizabeth A. Johnson, "Does God Play Dice? Divine Providence and Chance," *Theological Studies* 57.1 (1996): 5.

[9] Johnson, "Does God Play Dice?," p. 8.

[10] Polkinghorne, "Physics and Metaphysics in a Trinitarian Perspective," p. 42.

[11] Margaret J. Wheatley, *Leadership and the New Science: Learning about Organization from an Orderly Universe* (San Francisco, Ca.: Berrett-Koehler Publishers, 1992), pp. 75–99.

[12] Haught, "Evolution and God's Humility," p. 14.

[13] Haught, "Evolution and God's Humility," p. 15.

[14] Haught, "Evolution and God's Humility," p. 17.

[15] Jürgen Moltmann, *God in Creation: A New Theology of Creation and the Spirit of God*, Margaret Kohl, trans. (Minneapolis: Fortress, 1993), p. 76.

[16] Moltmann, *God in Creation*, pp. 86–88.

[17] John F. Haught, *Science and Religion: From Conflict to Conversation* (New York: Paulist, 1995), p. 161.

[18] Bonaventure, *Itin.* 6.2 (V, 310). Cousins, trans. *Bonaventure*, p. 103.

[19] See Ilia Delio, "Does God 'Act'? A Bonaventurian Response," *Heythrop Journal* 44.3 (July 2003): 328–344.

[20] Hayes, "Incarnation and Creation in St. Bonaventure," p. 314.

[21] Cousins, "Two Poles of St. Bonaventure's Theology," p. 161.

[22] See Delio, "Does God Act?," p. 337.

[23] Kevin P. Keane, "Why Creation? Bonaventure and Thomas Aquinas on God as Creative Good," *Downside Review* 93 (April 1975), pp. 117–119. Keane offers some interesting insights with regard to creation and divine goodness. He writes: "Bonaventure attempted to provide a more adequate answer to the 'why' of finite being...more in keeping with the

affirmation of creation's fittingness expressed in the Christian experience of the perfect Word/ Reason *(Logos)* as incarnate in Jesus of Nazareth." He goes on to say that "the fate of the world, for good or for ill, is of consequence to God, for his goodness is radically involved: he would not be the good itself, the best, were he to abandon the project once under way or complacently witness its disaster."

[24] Denis Edwards, *The God of Evolution* (New York: Paulist, 1999), p. 30.

[25] Hans Urs Von Balthasar, *Theo-Drama: Theological Dramatic Theory*, vol. I, *Prolegomena* (San Francisco: Ignatius Press, 1988), p. 20.

[26] Hans Urs Von Balthasar, *Theo-Drama: Theological Dramatic Theory*, vol. IV, *The Action* (San Francisco: Ignatius Press, 1994), p. 327.

[27] Edwards, *God of Evolution*, pp. 30–31.

[28] Edwards, *God of Evolution*, p 76.

[29] Jürgen Moltmann, "God's Kenosis in the Creation and Consummation of the World," in *Work of Love*, p. 147.

[30] See, for example, Arthur Peacocke, *Theology for a Scientific Age: Being and Becoming Natural, Divine, and Human* (Minneapolis: Fortress, 1993), pp. 53–54; and Philip Clayton, *God and Contemporary Science* (Grand Rapids, Mich.: Eerdmans, 1997), p. 227; Ian Barbour, "God's Power: A Process View," in *Work of Love*, p. 3.

[31] Moltmann, *God in Creation*, pp. 83–84. Moltmann writes: "It is more appropriate if we view the eternal divine life as a life of eternal, infinite love, which in the creative process issues in its overflowing rapture from its trinitarian perfection and completeness, and comes to itself in the eternal rest of sabbath" (p. 84). Moltmann goes on to say that the one divine love operates in different ways in the divine life and in the divine creativity, making possible the distinction between God and the world.

[32] Martin Buber, *I and Thou*, Roland Gregor Smith, trans. (New York: Scribner's, 1970), pp. 37–72.

[33] See Joseph A. Bracken, "Intersubjectivity and the Coming of God," *Journal of Religion* (2003): 397.

[34] The term "strange attractor," arising from chaos theory, describes the shape of chaos or spontaneous movements of a system that deviate from the normal pattern of order. The use of computer imagery has helped to detect spontaneous non-linear deviations in systems that signify new patterns of order. A strange attractor is a basin of attraction that pulls the system into a visible shape. It is, in some way, the spontaneous non-linear variation in a system that ultimately causes a new pattern of order to emerge. Some scientists have claimed that the appearance of the "strange attractor" means that order is inherent in chaos since the "attractor" itself is a novel pattern of order that arises spontaneously within a system. When systems are dislodged from a stable state, there is first a period of oscillation prior to a state of full chaos or a period of total unpredictability; it is during this time that the strange attractor seems to "spontaneously" appear. Very slight variations, so small as to be indiscernible, can amplify into unpredictable results when they are fed back on themselves. See Wheatley, *Leadership and the New Science*, p. 105; David Toolan, *At Home in the Cosmos* (Maryknoll, N.Y.: Orbis, 2000), p. 200.

[35] Keane (p. 116) suggests that Bonaventure's metaphysics of the good may have been influenced by his teachers in the theology faculty at Paris who, in their *Summa Fratris Alexandri*, suggested that we may be making a "cosmocentric" or "cosmo-morphic" error in assuming that goodness is secondary to being in the Godhead.

[36] Bonaventure, *Itin.* 6.5 (V, 310). Cousins, trans. *Bonaventure*, p. 107. This is Bonaventure's notion of the coincidence of opposites, which is a structure of thought that characterizes his theology.

[37] Moltmann, *God in Creation*, pp. 75–76.

[38] Haught, *Science and Religion*, p. 161.

[39] Walter Kasper, *The God of Jesus Christ*, Matthew J. O'Connell, trans. (New York: Crossroad, 1984), pp. 194–95.

[40] "The Little Flowers of Saint Francis," 11 in *Francis of Assisi: Early Documents*, vol. III, *The Prophet*, Regis J. Armstrong, J.A. Wayne Hellmann and William B. Short, eds. (New York: New City Press, 2001), p. 584. See also Jane Kopas, "A Franciscan Interpretation of Person in Postmodern Culture," in *Franciscan Identity and Postmodern Culture*, Kathleen A. Warren, ed. (New York: The Franciscan Institute, 2003), pp. 67–68.

Chapter Five

THE TEARS OF GOD

The SS hanged two Jewish men and a youth in front of the whole camp. The men died quickly, but the death throes of the youth lasted for half an hour. "Where is God? Where is he?" Someone asked behind me. As the youth still hung in torment in the noose after a long time, I heard the man call again, "Where is God now?" And I heard a voice in myself answer: "Where is he? He is here. He is hanging there on the gallows."
—Elie Wiesel, *Night*

The world is full of broken hearts because a heart can love and love is vulnerable. There are broken hearts scattered all over the world, in places of war, in dying children, in the frustrated faces of the unemployed and elderly. Yes, the heart is a vulnerable thing because it yearns to love. The human heart is just like the heart of God.

We live in a violent world, war upon war, destruction upon destruction. In just about every corner of the world, violence abounds. Human tears are so abundant in parts of the world that sadness is the face of daily life. We often shut down in the face of human misery because we feel our helplessness, our weakness, our inability to act. It is easier sometimes not to show emotion than to join in the human valley of tears. It is easier to live privately than to be involved in the pain of others. As one television commercial reminds us, "who has time for pain?" The answer in our Western culture is, "no one." We do not have time for pain or suffering or any type of disorder in the human condition and, because we have no time, pain and suffering abound. If we could only realize that suffering and death are part of the greater fullness of life, we would run to embrace them for that is what we seek, the fullness of life. If we could only realize that suffering and death are part of God's creation, we would accept them, for we desire to become a new creation. If we knew that pain and suffering touch the heart of God, we would allow them to touch us as well, for what we seek is God's heart of love. But since we have closed our minds to these truths, pain and suffering prevail.

It is difficult enough that we humans, especially in Western culture, are immune to the pain and suffering of the world but how about God? Is God affected by the suffering of the world? Is the good news of Jesus Christ really "good" news in a world of sorrow? One could say that a God of humble love who allows violence, suffering and death to be part of life is a disinterested God, a God who does not want to get involved with a messy world. We could assume that a humble God is an impotent God, a God who is defenseless and vulnerable—in short, a God who really cannot save us from the perils of destruction. But a disinterested God is not a hopeful God. It is the God of deists, the God of modernity, the God who can and has been easily pushed out of the world. The God of Francis and Bonaventure is different. Theirs is a God who is so bent low in love for *every* creature and all creation that God goes to the depth of human suffering—the cross—to show his love and to bring all those in darkness into the embrace of love. To live in relation to Francis' God, to be God-like, is to participate in the sufferings of the world, to be compassionate.

While our post-Freudian age views pain and pleasure as psychic opposites, Francis, like other mystics of his age, viewed suffering as a participation in the suffering of God. In her book *Virgin Time*, the contemporary writer Patricia Hampl writes, "he [Francis] was a joyous mystic who *needed* to suffer the great pain of his age, because not to suffer, especially to miss out on the suffering of the world, was not to live."[1] Francis lived in a time when there was great emphasis on literal imitation of the poor and suffering Christ. Starvation, illness, solidarity with the poor and sick were means of identifying with Christ on the cross. As Caroline Bynum writes, "becoming Christ physically was a way of being snatched up into his divinity."[2] While our contemporary Western culture still tends to separate matter from spirit as if these natures have little in common, the medieval mind saw matter and spirit united in the human person, particularly in Jesus Christ. The body was seen as the locus of the divine. It is in this respect that we can understand suffering in the life of Francis, especially in relation to love.

For the Franciscans, love and suffering form the pathway into God. To understand God's involvement in a world of sorrow, at least from a Franciscan perspective, is to consider how love intertwines with suffering in the crucified Christ. In his youth, Francis, like many people, rejected the sick and poor of society. "The sight of lepers," Thomas of Celano claimed, "was so bitter to him that in the days of his vanity when he saw their houses even two miles away, he would cover his nose with his hands."[3] However, Francis had a change of heart and one day he met a leper along the road. Instead of turning away, Francis came up and kissed the leper, gave the leper alms and went away. What made Francis kiss the leper? What makes anyone kiss a leper? The answer is not apparent but we are given insight through Francis' experience of the crucified Christ. One day Francis wandered into the dilapidated church of San Damiano. Standing before a Byzantine cross depicting Christ crucified and glorified, Francis' heart was stricken and wounded with melting love and compassion for the passion of Christ; and for the rest of his life he carried in it the wounds of the Lord Jesus.[4] Francis was touched deeply by the compassionate love of God, a God visibly bent over in love in the wounds of Jesus Christ. "Because of Christ crucified," Bonaventure wrote, Francis "showed deeds of humility and humanity to lepers with a gentle piety.... To poor beggars he even wished to give not only his possessions but his very self, sometimes taking off his clothes, at others altering them, at yet others, when he had nothing else at hand, ripping them in pieces to give to them."[5] Touched deeply by the compassionate love of God in the wounded flesh of Christ, Francis became the compassion of God in the world.

Mary Jo Meadows defines compassion as "the quivering of the heart in response to another's suffering."[6] Compassion is the ability to "get inside the skin of another" in order to respond with loving concern and care. Compassion is so deep and closely connected to others that the truly loving person breathes in the pain of the world and breathes out compassion. The compassionate person identifies with the suffering of others in such a way that she or he makes a space within the heart, a womb of mercy, to allow suffering persons inside and to embrace them with arms of love. What we see in the life of Francis is that compassion begins with God who is humbly bent over in love in the cross of Jesus Christ. Love is the power of God that embraces fragile suffering humanity and transforms death into life.

There are many theologians today who speculate as to whether or not God suffers. Is God affected by the suffering of this world or not? In the early church, it was a heresy to believe that God suffers. A God who is perfect and immutable could not be subject to change. While theology affirmed that "God was in Christ" it was believed that Christ suffered in his human nature but not in his divine nature.[7] For the church Fathers, even to say that "God is love" did not betray a vulnerable God but a God whose action of *goodwill* is directed to other persons. True love was to will and achieve the good of another, not to have emotions. The impassible nature of God made it impossible for God to share in the sufferings of humanity. Augustine, for example, distinguished between emotions and moral actions with regard to the perfect love of God. He wrote: "His pity is not the wretched heart of a fellow-sufferer...the pity of God is the goodness of his help... when God pities, he does not grieve and he liberates."[8] Thomas Aquinas asserted that love, like joy but unlike sadness or anger, can be simply an act of the will and the intellect. Love can be ascribed to God as a purely intellectual capacity.[9] Yet, the impervious God of the church Fathers was not the God of the Old Testament, a God who suffers because of his covenant-love (*hesed*) for his people. The prophets of the Old Testament spoke of a God who grieves, is disappointed and labors under the burden of rejected love. The prophet Hosea, for example, writes:

> When Israel was a child I loved him, / and I called my son
> out of Egypt. / ...I myself taught Ephraim to walk, / I took
> them in my arms; / yet they have not understood that I

was the one looking after them. / I led them with reins of
kindness, / with leading-strings of love. / I was like someone
who lifts an infant close against his cheek; / stooping down
to him I gave him his food. (Hosea 11:1–5)

Could the God of Hosea really be a God who is immune to the suffering of humanity? A God who cannot feel the pain of loss or grief? Is
this not a God who is so close that he stoops down to feed us? Francis
of Assisi, like the prophet Hosea, experienced the God of *hesed*, a
God of such compassionate love that he bends low to press us to his
cheek. The God of Francis, like the God of Hosea, is not the God of
the intellectuals but a God who is so involved with his creation that
it is impossible to speculate about the suffering of God apart from the
suffering of creatures.

Francis and Bonaventure discovered a God of passionate love
revealed to us in the cross of Jesus Christ. To understand the significance of the cross for Bonaventure is to understand the Trinity of love.
Love, as we said before, is expressive. The love of the Father expresses
itself in the Son who is Word. The self-gift of the Father to the Son
reflects a self-emptying already within the heart of God in such a way
that we may think of the cross first in the heart of God before it is in
the heart of creation. The very act of creation reflects something of
a "divine crucifixion," for in creation God reveals his power to be his
unconditional love for the world. The act of descending into what
is nothing (creation) in order to express himself, according to Von
Balthasar, is God's humility, his condescension, his going outside his
own riches to become poor.[10] The cross is key not only to sin and
human nature, but to God himself. The cross reveals to us the heart
of God because it reveals the vulnerability of God's love. Balthasar
writes: "It is God's going forth into the danger and the nothingness of
the creation that reveals [God's] heart to be at its origin vulnerable; in
the humility of this vulnerability lies God's condescension [humility]
and thus his fundamental readiness to go to the very end of love on
the cross."[11] For Bonaventure, the mystery of the cross is the mystery
of poverty because here God is not possessing but fully communicating

the mystery of love in his radical openness to and acceptance of the human person. The poverty of the cross is one with and identical to the mystery of ecstatic divine love; it is an overflowing of love.[12] The passion is the revelation of the heart of God in the heart of Jesus disclosing the mystery of the cross as the overflowing fountain of God's love. That is why the mystery of cruciform love of the Son leads us into the very heart of the mystery of God. For the Trinity of love is poured out in the mystery of the crucified Christ and only through the mystery of Christ do we enter into the heart of the Trinity. Bonaventure described the fountain of God's love in the cross particularly in his spiritual writings. In his letter to Poor Clare nuns, for example, he writes:

> Indeed, no sorrow was ever comparable to Yours, O Lord Jesus Christ! Your blood was shed so abundantly that Your whole body was soaked with it...why did You let Your blood pour forth in a river when a single drop would have sufficed for the redemption of the world? I know, Lord, I know in all truth that you did this for no other reason than to show the depth of Your love for me![13]

The cross signifies the wedding between God and humanity. God betrothes himself forever to us precisely in and through suffering and death:

> Christ on the cross bows his head waiting for you, that he may kiss you; His arms outstretched, that he may embrace you, his hands are open, that he may enrich you; his body spread out, that he may give himself totally; his feet are nailed, that he may stay there; his side is open for you, that he may let you enter there.[14]

With arms outstretched, the kiss and embrace of Christ in a broken world is the fullest expression of the humility of God. The cross signifies to us that God is vulnerable in love. God takes a risk in loving us and invites us into his love. And he does this in such a visible way that we would have to ask, what kind of lover would God be if God's love remained untouched by the sufferings of humanity? Thus, Bonaventure describes a God of love who becomes submerged in the waters of human suffering in order to embrace in love:

See, now, my soul,
how he who is God *blessed above all things,*
Is totally submerged
in the waters of suffering
from *the sole of the foot to the top of the head.*
In order that he might draw you out totally
from these sufferings,
The waters have come up to his soul...
And then transfixed
with nails,
he appeared to you as your beloved
cut through with wound upon wound
In order to heal you.
Who will grant me...
what I long for...
I may be fixed
with my beloved
to the yoke of the cross?[15]

For Bonaventure the humility of God is expressed most fully as the power of God's love in and through suffering and death. The centrality of the cross signifies a God who is radically involved with the world and ultimately concerned for the world's completion in love. Gregory Baum helps elucidate Bonaventure's position on divine suffering when he states that suffering can have two meanings. On one hand, suffering is due to a lack of something that belongs to our integrity. We suffer because we are personally vulnerable: we can lose our health, our family, our friends, our job and anything else that is precious to us. This type of suffering may be called suffering *ex carentia* (by deprivation). However we may also suffer because our friends or family are vulnerable: our heart is torn because they have lost something that belongs to their integrity. We suffer with them because we have extended to them our love and our solidarity; we suffer with them because we have reached beyond ourselves and identified ourselves with them; we suffer because an inner wealth or fullness has allowed us to give ourselves away. Baum calls this suffering *ex abundantia* (out of fullness). Suffering *ex abundantia* is compassion. Thus while God cannot suffer *ex carentia* since God cannot lose what pertains to God's integrity, God can (and does) suffer *ex abundantia*: out of the divine plenitude God loves those who suffer, shares their pain, and bears their burdens with them.[16]

Bonaventure describes God's participation in suffering as a participation *ex abundantia*. Out of the fountain fullness of God's humble self-giving love, God shares in the pain and suffering of the world. This is a God who gets so "foolishly close" that the boundaries between what is human and what is sacred become blurry.[17] Suffering is not the consequence of sin but the place of transformation. It is a door by which God can enter in and love us where we are, in our human weakness, our misery and our pain. When we let go of our defenses, our egos and our walls of separation God can embrace us in the fragile flesh of our humanity. As Clare of Assisi realized, God bends down in the cross to share our tears out of a heart full of mercy and love—and we are caught up in his embrace.

The power of God is the powerlessness of God's unconditional love shown to us in the cross. God is the beggar who will not force his way into our homes unless we open the door. God is with us at every moment with open arms of love, laughing when we are laughing, weeping when we are weeping, rejoicing when we are rejoicing. God shares in the brokenness of this world out of the abundance of divine love. It is because God is the fountain fullness of love, in Bonaventure's view, that God can share in the sufferings of our lives and through these sufferings draw us into new life. For God's love cannot be overcome by human power nor can it be conquered by human force. God's love, shown to us in the weakness and powerlessness of the cross, is the power of love to heal and transform death into life. God is most God-like in the suffering of the cross. It is in this respect that the ringing words of Dietrich Bonhoeffer, in his famous letter of July 16, 1944, hold true:

God lets himself be pushed out of the world on to the cross.

> He is weak and powerless in the world, and that is precisely
> the way, the only way, in which he is with us and helps
> us.... The Bible directs man to God's powerlessness and
> suffering; only the suffering God can help.[18]

To have faith in a God of unconditional love is to realize how intimately close God is. So close that our joys and sorrows, our grief and
anguish are wrapped up tightly in God's humble embrace. So close we
forget God's presence. In his own day, Jesus was immersed in a violent
culture, a culture of conflict and anxiety. But he also knew of the deeper
truth hidden beneath the surface of human judgment, namely, that this
broken, anxious world is oozing with God. He asked us to have faith,
to believe that the reign of God is among us and within us. As Patrick
Malone writes:

> Faith is more than a magical formula to conquer the worry,
> regret, shame and resentments that cloud our visions and
> make us jaded and tired. Having faith does not remove
> every trace of self-absorption and doubt. Those things are
> part of the human condition. Faith is what brings us into
> the deepest truth...that says we are in the image of an
> unlimited, unrestricted, unimaginable love. And when we
> forget that, as Jesus reminded the religious authorities of his
> day, then religion does become a shield, a crutch, a closed
> refuge instead of a way to boldly throw ourselves into a
> harsh world, knowing that is precisely where we discover
> a generous God.[19]

In his spiritual writings Bonaventure indicated that in *this* world, suffering is God's way of being involved with the significant other of his
love—creation—because suffering is the most authentic expression
and communication of love. There is no other path into the heart of
God, Bonaventure wrote, than through the burning love of the crucified Christ.[20] There is no real love without suffering and there is no
real suffering where there is love. The person who cannot love cannot
suffer, for she or he is without grief, without feeling and indifferent. As

Dorothee Söelle suggests, "When a being who is free from suffering is worshipped as God, then it is possible to train oneself in patience, endurance, imperturbability, and aloofness from suffering."[21] Apathy, Söelle writes, is the sickness of our times, a sickness of persons and systems, a sickness to death.[22] To find in the pain of human weakness the liberation of love and to love by accepting human weakness is the path to God. For suffering is overcome by suffering and wounds are healed by wounds. We suffer when we experience in suffering the lack of love, the pain of abandonment and the powerlessness of unbelief. The suffering of pain and abandonment is overcome by the suffering of love, which is not afraid of what is sick and ugly but accepts it and takes it into itself to heal it. Anyone who enters into love, and through love experiences the inextricable suffering and the fatality of death, enters into the history of the human God. In the suffering and death of Jesus we find the power to love in the midst of suffering because love is stronger than death. The more one loves, therefore, the more one is open to sorrow. When at the end of his life Francis of Assisi beheld the vision of the crucified man, he was flooded with a mixture of joy and sorrow. "He rejoiced at the gracious way Christ looked upon him," Bonaventure wrote, "but the fact that He was fastened to a cross *pierced his soul with a sword* of compassionate sorrow."[23]

It is in the mixture of joy and sorrow that love finds a home in the universe. All of nature is cruciform, Holmes Rolston writes, "this whole evolutionary upslope is a calling in which renewed life comes by blasting the old. Life is gathered up in the midst of its throes, a blessed tragedy, lived in grace through a besetting storm."[24] We are called to let go and enter into the storm, to love as passionately, extravagantly and wastefully as God has loved us. We are called into the fullness of our humanity through the crucified Christ. In light of the cruciform nature of creation Rolston writes:

> The abundant life that Jesus exemplifies and offers to his
> disciples is that of a sacrificial suffering through to some-
> thing higher. The Spirit of God is the genius that makes
> alive, that redeems life from its evils. The cruciform creation

is, in the end, deiform, godly, just because of this element of struggle, not in spite of it. There is a great divine "yes" hidden behind and within every "no" of crushing nature. God…is the compassionate lure in, with, and under all purchasing of life at the cost of sacrifice. Long before humans arrived, the way of nature was already a via dolorosa. In that sense, the aura of the cross is cast backward across the whole global story, and it forever outlines the future.… *The capacity to suffer through to joy* is a supreme emergent and an essence of Christianity.[25]

"To suffer through to joy" is to accept death as the path into life. In the last chapter of his *Soul's Journey into God* Bonaventure states that only those who love death can see God. By "death" he means that we are to let go into God, to allow the dominance of God's grace invade our lives. For the intellectual mind can never behold the depth of God. Only the heart can enter into the incomprehensible mystery of divine love.

That is why it is hard to explain logically a religion where we have a God who gets absurdly close, so incredibly close that we are forced to discover the face of God in all the mess of creation, no matter how confusing or abrasive.[26] Too often we want a God who will hear our cries, who will be strong enough to push our experiences away. It is not that God is deaf to the cry of the poor. It is rather that God himself weeps. God himself is poor. The poor one cries out to the poor God and the poor God answers, "I am here!" Only a humble God who bends so low to throw it all away in love can heal us and make us whole. This "bending low" of God, this "foolish nearness" of God, says to us that God lives in human hearts. God's compassion needs human hands, human eyes and human touch. We who are incarnational people are called to be the compassionate love of God. "There is only one action believers can perform and not be accused of arrogance, naïveté or delusion," Malone writes. "Our only credible action is to bless this world, not by conquering our failures but by allowing God to break through our less-than-stellar lives."[27] We have enormous power to heal this wounded world through the power of compassionate love, that love which is not afraid of what is sick and ugly but accepts the suffering of frail humanity and embraces it as its own. The power of God's healing love belongs to us if we choose to accept its demands.

Francis of Assisi became known as a "second Christ" because his life exemplified the compassionate love of God. He did not wait for people to come to him nor did he reject the sick and the poor. On the contrary, he went out to meet people where they were, on the margins of society, realizing that letting go of the self-centered ego is the only path to real union in love. Francis was not afraid to love through suffering for the sake of healing relationships. There is a story recounted in one of the legends that speaks of Francis' solidarity in love. According to the legend, a simple brother by the name of James had taken a leper covered with sores outside the hospital where he was ministering to the lepers. Francis saw what James was doing and rebuked him for his actions. Afterwards, Francis reproached himself for reprimanding James because he felt that in reproving Brother James he had shamed the leper. To amend for his actions, Francis brought the leper in to eat with him. The author writes:

> While blessed Francis was sitting at the table with the leper and other brothers, a bowl was placed between the two of them. The leper was completely covered with sores and ulcerated, and especially the fingers with which he was eating were deformed and bloody, so that whenever he put them in the bowl, blood dripped into it.[28]

The story may shock us but it also causes us to consider the cost of healing love. What are we willing to suffer so that love might heal the wounds of humanity and transform them into the glory of God? Only when we can exit our private lives and enter into the pain and misery of others does the cross take on meaning as the transformative power of God's love. God bends low to love us where we are and suffers with us out of a heart full of mercy. But we can know this love only in human form. God does not need perfect creatures to show his power. God needs selfless vessels to pour out his selfless compassionate love. We are invited into the mystery of God's incomprehensible love, a love that is revealed in the powerlessness of human suffering and death in the cross. To accept this invitation is to profess belief in a bountiful, kind God, a God of overflowing and humble love. God's tears glisten on the fragile human face, the flawed creature who stumbles through the world in search of goodness. God is with us and his glory radiates when we strive to love by bearing the wounds of love. The crucified Christ is risen and glorified. God's tears are mixed with joy. We do not have to worry whether or not God suffers with us. Rather we are to realize that our suffering is already caught up in the suffering of God, the outward moving, overflowing love of the Father for the Son. Only in this way is God our hope and the future of life.

REFLECTION QUESTIONS

1. How do you view suffering in your life? Do you get angry with God? Do you blame God for your suffering? Or do you view suffering as an invitation to deeper love?

2. How much of your life are you willing to spend in love? Do you believe in "costly discipleship"? Are you willing to risk your life for the sake of love?

3. How does relationship with a God of humble love empower you to accept life's sufferings with courage?

NOTES

[1] Patricia Hampl, *Virgin Time: In Search of the Contemplative Life* (New York: Farrar, Straus, Giroux, 1992), p. 121.

[2] Caroline Walker Bynum, *Holy Feast and Holy Fast: The Religious Significance of Food to Medieval Women* (Berkeley, Ca.: University of California Press, 1987), p. 258.

[3] "The Life of Saint Francis by Thomas of Celano," 7 in *FA:ED* I, p. 195.

[4] "The Legend of the Three Companions" 5 in *FA:ED* II, p. 76.

[5] Bonaventure, "The Major Legend of Saint Francis," 1.6 in *FA:ED* II, p. 534.

[6] Cited in Joyce Rupp, *The Cup of Our Life: A Guide for Spiritual Growth* (Notre Dame, Ind.: Ave Maria Press, 1997), p. 110.

[7] Paul S. Fiddes, *The Creative Suffering of God* (Oxford: Clarendon Press, 1988), pp. 27–29.

[8] Augustine, *Contra Adversarium Legis et Prophetarum* 1.40 cited in Fiddes, *Creative Suffering of God*, p. 17.

[9] Thomas Aquinas, *Summa Theologia* 1a. 20, 1 cited in Fiddes, *Creative Suffering of God*, p. 18.

[10] Hans Urs Von Balthasar, *The Glory of the Lord: Theological Aesthetics*, Andrew Louth, Francis McDonagh and Brian McNeil, trans., vol. II, *Studies in Theological Style: Clerical Styles*, Joseph Fessio, ed. (San Francisco, Ca.: Ignatius Press, 1984), p. 353.

[11] Balthasar, *The Glory of the Lord*, p. 356.

[12] J.A. Wayne Hellmann, "Poverty: The Franciscan Way to God," *Theology Digest* 22 (1974): 341.

[13] Bonaventure, *De perfectione vitae ad sorores* 6.6 (VIII, 122) "On the Perfection of Life, Addressed to Sisters." José de Vinck, trans. (Paterson, N.J.: St. Anthony Guild Press, 1960), p. 243.

[14] Bonaventure *Soliloquium* 1.39 (VIII, 41) *Soliloquy*, vol. II, *Mystical Opuscula*. Jose de Vinck, trans. (Paterson, N.J.: St. Anthony Guild Press, 1966), p. 69.

[15] Bonaventure, *Lig. vit.* 26 (VIII, 78). Cousins, trans., *Bonaventure*, pp. 148–149. It should be noted here that Bonaventure followed the medieval distinction between divine and human suffering. In his *Breviloquium* he states that the divine nature did not suffer; however, in his humanity (flesh) Christ suffered physically and spiritually; however, his Christology here also follows Anselm's satisfaction theory. See Bonaventure, *Breviloquium* 9.1 (V, 238). Bonaventure's Christology develops in later spiritual writings, and I would suggest that his understanding of God's relation to suffering humanity also changes. The distinction between divine and human suffering becomes less formal. The difference between suffering out of the fullness of love and suffering out of need, as I discuss in the text, corresponds more appropriately to Bonaventure's emphasis on the crucified Christ and the relationship of God to suffering humanity.

[16] Gregory Baum, "Meister Eckhart and Dorothee Soëlle on Suffering and the Experience of God," in *Light Burdens, Heavy Blessings* (Quincy, Ill.: Franciscan Press, 2000), pp. 235–236.

[17] Patrick Malone, "A God Who Gets Foolishly Close," *America* (May 27, 2000): 22.

[18] Dietrich Bonhoeffer, *Letters and Papers from Prison*, Eberhard Bethge, ed. (New York: Macmillan, 1972), p. 360.

[19] Malone, "A God Who Gets Foolishly Close," p. 22.

[20] This is Bonaventure's central idea in his *Soul's Journey into God* (*Itinerarium*). See *Itin.* prol. 3 (V, 295).

[21] See Fiddes, *Creative Suffering of God*, p. 48.

[22] Dorothee Söelle, *Suffering*, Everett R. Kalin, trans. (Philadelphia: Fortress, 1975), pp. 36–59; Lucien Richard, *What Are They Saying About the Theology of Suffering?* (New York: Paulist, 1992), pp. 76–77.

[23] Bonaventure, "The Major Legend of Saint Francis," 13.3 in *FA:ED* II, p. 632.

[24] Holmes Rolston III, "Kenosis and Nature," in *The Work of Love*, p. 59.

[25] Rolston, "Kenosis and Nature," in *The Work of Love*, pp. 59–60. Emphasis added.

[26] Malone, "A God Who Gets Foolishly Close," p. 23.

[27] Malone, "A God Who Gets Foolishly Close," p. 23.

[28] "The Assisi Compilation," in *FA:ED* II, p. 167.

Chapter Six

THE FACE OF GOD

What if God was one of us
Just a slob like one of us
Just a stranger on the bus
Trying to make his way home
—Sung by Joan Osborne, written by Eric M. Bazilian,
"One of Us"

We live in a world of many differences. I moved to the Washington, D.C., area eight years ago and it didn't take me long to realize that white, western men and women of European descent are no longer the co-creators of American culture. In the apartment building where I reside there are Ethiopians, Indians, Africans, Mexicans and Philippinos among others, all of whom are American citizens or are in the process of obtaining citizenship. I was particularly struck one day last Christmas when I got on the elevator and met my Ethiopian neighbors—husband, wife and two children—all loaded with presents, singing "Jingle Bells." Another Ethiopian family on the ground floor of our building led a "house church" for several years in their apartment. Members came from all over every week (judging by the lack of available parking spaces on "church evenings") and gathered in the small living room of this young couple. For hours on end (and, I might add, with full voice) they would sing and pray. On Sundays the women (and men) came in their traditional attire for the community meal and celebration. I was very impressed by the number of people gathered for these communal events, as if family was what community is all about.

Teaching theology in a metropolitan area of cultural and religious diversity impels one to consider the meaning of Christ in a new way. It is difficult to believe anymore that Christ belongs only to Catholics or that Christ lives only in a golden tabernacle or that Christ has nothing to do with the unbaptized or those who do not know Christ. Moreover, it is difficult to believe that Christ has nothing to do with creation and appeared only after fifteen billion years of evolution. What kind of an incarnate God are we talking about anyway? Such beliefs vindicate a very small God, not a God of infinite compassionate love, but a God who counts the cost of things and works on a fixed schedule. Such a God could not be humbly bent low in love for *all* creation.

When we talk about the Incarnation we are talking about the Word of God made flesh, as well as the potential within creation to receive the divine Word into it. The evolutionary universe has an ancient history of expanding and unfolding life that has culminated in the emergence of the human person. All along, we might say, Incarnation, Word made flesh, has been happening in the universe. That Word, however, comes to the fullest and most perfect expression in the human person of Jesus Christ. Incarnation, therefore, is not about who is baptized or unbaptized or who may be lost versus who may be saved. Rather, it is first about the Word through whom the whole creation unfolds and in whom all of creation finds its ultimate meaning. The Incarnation is not a card-carrying club membership; it is the culmination of the potential within the universe to be united to God. It is creation's "yes" to the infinite love of God. Everything that exists, all of created reality, finds its meaning in relation to the Incarnate Word of God, Jesus Christ.

It is sometimes confusing to talk about Christ and not Jesus of Nazareth, as if we are talking about a cosmic principle and a human person. While many of us know the story of Jesus of Nazareth and are inspired by his selfless love, mercy and compassion, still I wonder how many of us think that Jesus was from Nazareth and Christ was his last name, as if Jesus might have been the son of "Mr. and Mrs. Christ"? What is the relation between the earthly man Jesus and Jesus the Christ, that is, the anointed one of God? Here is the key to understanding the Christ mystery in an evolutionary world and our role as

Christians in this mystery.

When we say that Christ, the Word of God, is the meaning of the whole creation, we are saying that Christ is the Word through whom all things are made. Thus, everything in some way expresses God as a little word of God because it is created through the one divine Word. However, the divine Word is most fully and perfectly expressed in the person of Jesus of Nazareth who, as the perfectly expressed Word, is divine and yet fully human. As human, Jesus is intimately united to the whole created world. When Jesus died on the cross, resurrected and ascended into heaven, it was not only the individual, human person Jesus who went to God (as if he made it and left the rest of us behind) but it was the divine Word—the One through whom everything is created—incarnate in the person of Jesus who underwent death, resurrection and ascension into heaven. Thus, in the person of Jesus Christ, the Word incarnate, all of humanity and creation is taken up into the life of God in such a way that Christ is now present to every person and all creation as the one who mediates our relationship to the infinite source of divine love. Because Jesus, the Word incarnate, conquered death by death and now lives at the right hand of the Father, he is confessed as the "Christ," the Messiah, the One sent by God for the salvation (healing and wholeness) of the universe. When we say, therefore, that Christ is the meaning of the whole creation we are saying that Jesus *is* the Christ but Christ is more than the man Jesus because Christ is the Word incarnate, crucified and glorified, the One in whom every person (no matter what their religion, race, culture or creed) and all creation (stars, birds and lilacs) bear an intimate relationship with God. The import of this statement is profound and it would take a lifetime of prayer to really plumb this mystery, but for our purposes let me turn to Bonaventure and Scotus to help realize the significance of Jesus Christ as the meaning of creation.

The root of the Christ mystery, according to Bonaventure, is the Trinity. Here we find the Word as the full expression of the Father's self-diffusive goodness. When we say that Christ is first in God's intention to love, as Scotus did, we mean that from all eternity God willed to love a finite other as a more perfect expression of his love. Creation is already included in the otherness of God's love from all eternity because of Christ. This relates to what we said in chapter three, namely, that creation is caught up in the infinite loving relationships of the Father, Son and Spirit. For Bonaventure, Incarnation and creation are two sides of the same coin, so to speak. Creation is not radically separate from God but a finite expression of the infinite Word of God. Bonaventure did not perceive the cosmic Christ as an impersonal, abstract principle or a mathematical formula. Rather, the cosmic significance of Christ is related to the way the eternal, creative and revelatory Word of God has emerged in human experience, namely, through the history of Jesus. When God creates, he can do so only "in and through the Word" of his own otherness, so that whatever created reality exists appears as the external otherness that is placed through the immanent otherness. There is only one Word of God and that Word spoken in history is Christ. God creates with a view toward Christ because Christ is the goal of creation, the object of God's love from all eternity.

When we understand that Christ gives meaning and purpose to creation, we see that Incarnation is more than about ridding us of sin. As Zachary Hayes writes, Christ is not an afterthought on the part of God.[1] Rather, God's primary purpose for becoming Incarnate is grounded in the divine desire to love, to be our beginning and our end, to be "God with us," in order that we might dwell in the presence of the divine. In this way, Christ is not an intrusion into an otherwise evolutionary universe. Rather, the whole process of evolution points to Christ. Margaret Pirkl indicates that the universe is an external embodiment of the inner Word of God; thus, there is something incarnational throughout the whole creation.[2] In the Incarnation itself there is a perfect fit between Christ and creation because everything has been made to resemble Christ. In a lecture on Franciscan theology Bill Short claimed that "before anything is poured out as creation, what God is expressing is what this body of Christ is: when Jesus comes as the Incarnation of God, there is a perfect fit, because everything has been made to resemble Jesus Christ."[3] Bonaventure says that the deepest truth about the created world is that it has within itself the potential to become, through God's grace, something of what it has already come to be in the mystery of Christ. In the life of Jesus of Nazareth, creation's "yes" to the fullness of God's love is realized, and in his death and resurrection, all of creation becomes what it was always intended to be, the Beloved of the infinite love of God. Thus, what happened between God and Christ points to the future of the cosmos. It is a future that involves a radical transformation of created reality through the unitive power of God's love.[4]

The idea that Christ is first in God's intention to love takes on a deeper meaning when we consider it in relation to Bonaventure's notion of the coincidence of opposites.[5] According to Bonaventure, the coincidence of opposites is rooted in the Trinity itself, particularly in the divine person of the Father. Because the Father is without origin or has no "beginning," he is fecund and self-communicative. The self-communicative goodness of the Father is expressed in the Son and Spirit. Whereas the Son is both generated by the Father and with the Father generates the Spirit, the Spirit is totally receptive to the Father's love. Within the Trinity, therefore, are the opposites of the Father and Spirit united by the Son who is center. In his *Soul's Journey into God* Bonaventure indicates that the Trinity of opposites is expressed in the mystery of Christ who, as Word of God and center of the Trinity, is the perfect coincidence of opposites. He writes:

> When our mind contemplates
> in Christ the Son of God
> ... it sees united
> the first and the last,
> the highest and the lowest,
> the circumference and the center,
> the Alpha and the Omega,
> the caused and the cause,
> the Creator and the creature...[6]

Christ is the union of infinite and finite, eternal and temporal, divine and human, Creator and creature. When the human mind contemplates God in Christ, Bonaventure states, it attains perfect contemplation insofar as we cannot know anything more of God.

Throughout his writings, Bonaventure proclaimed that Christ is the center: the center of the soul, the center of creation, the center of the universe, the center of all time and history. All lines of creation emanate and converge in Christ the center. For Bonaventure, the centrality of Christ is not a unifying principle that erases the differences between religions or between peoples. Rather, the centrality of Christ is the body of Christ in the diversity of its members. Ewert Cousins says that the entire spatio-temporal cosmos is centered in Christ and every person is related to Christ as the cosmic center. Christ is the one person who embodies the whole creation and the whole creation—its content, meaning and purpose—is summarized in Christ. Thus, for the fullness of the Christ mystery we must look to the entire cosmos. Only in the diversity of religions and peoples is the fullness of the Christ mystery revealed.[7] How do we come to live in relationship to this Christ of creation, the Christ of all peoples, the Christ who is center and goal of the universe? We can find some clues in the life of Francis of Assisi, as Bonaventure reflected on his life.

Bonaventure views the life of Francis as a growth in awareness of divine goodness at the heart of the world in and through the mystery of Christ. His story is framed by Francis' encounter with the crucified Christ. In encountering Christ crucified Francis met the God of humble love. This meeting became the basis of encountering God in the particularity of every other where the humility of God was expressed in ordinary human flesh. Bonaventure describes Francis' initial encounter with Christ in the brokendown church of San Damiano where he highlights Christ's appearance to Francis in the visible form of the cross. He writes: "His [Francis'] *soul melted* at the sight, and the memory of Christ's passion was so impressed on the innermost recesses of his heart."[8] This encounter with the Other, crucified/God, changes Francis in the very core of his being. "From then on," Bonaventure claims, "he clothed himself with a spirit of poverty, a sense of humility, and an eagerness for intimate piety."[9] The expression of God's love in the self-emptying of the cross impressed Francis in such a way that what was loathsome to him, namely, the sight of lepers, became the object of his love. Impressed by Christ's love, Francis could no longer remain alone in his search for God. Rather, he found God in relation to the other. The necessity of the other for Francis thrust him into radical poverty whereby everything that hindered his relation to the other was stripped away. The encounter with Christ as other, therefore, imparted to Francis a new openness and freedom. Embraced by the compassionate love of God, Francis was liberated within and went out to embrace the other in love. By experiencing God's love in the visible figure of the Crucified, Francis became a man of true relationship.

For Bonaventure, Francis was the truly human one because he found himself not to be a self-isolated subject but a self that is essentially related to the other. Through his encounter with Christ, Francis came to accept all others as truly worthy of his love. Christ is the Word of God and in that first encounter with Christ, Francis was impressed by the Word in such a way that his life radically changed. No longer held bound by the things of this world, he was able to turn away from self-concern and from the ego's grasp, and pass over into the infinite goodness of God. The French philosopher Emmanuel Levinas states that the saint is the one who is totally at the disposal of the other and lives this exposure as response to the other by stripping the self of its "egoity" or, we might say, the need to project oneself onto the other.[10] In this way the other is seen as an excess, the "more" of what eludes the intellectual grasp. The face of the genuine other releases us from all desire for totality and opens us to a true sense of the infinite because inscribed in the face of the other is the trace of a transcendence.[11]

David Tracy points out that postmodern spirituality exposes the unreality of the modern subject's self-understanding as grounded in itself. Otherness, difference and excess are alternatives to the deadening sameness, the totalizing system, the security of the modern self-grounding subject.[12] In the life of Francis, Bonaventure indicates that Francis finds his identity in the other, first in relation to Christ, and then in the poor and sick.[13] Christ is the true light in whom Francis discovers his true self. Naming the truth of his own person before God allowed Francis to become free to make the journey to the other and back again.[14] Only in relation to the other did his weaknesses become strengths; for it was in naming his weaknesses that Francis matured in authentic human love. Because of the mystery of Christ, Francis' personhood developed, from a self-centered "I" to a relational self, an "I" in need of a "Thou." The deeper he grew in relationship with Christ, the deeper he grew in relationship with others. As Francis deepened his relationship with Christ, the other became less outside Francis as object and more related to him as brother. In the life of Francis, Bonaventure highlights the idea that the one who dwells in Christ dwells in the other, because the fullness of who we are in Christ can only be found in the other. Thomas Merton wrote that only in union with Christ, who is the fully integrated Person, can one become trans-personal, trans- cultural and trans-social.[15] Only in union with Christ, the One, can a person be united to the many since, as Word and center of the Trinity, Christ is both the One and the Many. The difference of the other, therefore, was not an obstacle for Francis but rather a celebration of God. For he found his identity in God, and he found God in the ordinary, fragile human flesh of the other.

Francis' discovery of relatedness was not limited to humans alone. He also found himself related to the tiny creatures of creation. Bonaventure wrote that "he [Francis] would call creatures, / no matter how small, / by the name of 'brother' or 'sister' / because he knew they shared with him the same beginning."[16] Everything in creation spoke to Francis of God. Just as he was impressed by the compassionate love of God in his encounter with the Crucified, so too he came to see that same love impressed on every level of creation. Francis found himself in a familial relationship with creation calling out to "brother lamb," "sister birds" and "sister cricket." On the level of creation, therefore, as on the level of humanity, Francis realized his relationship to others because of his intimate relationship to Christ. The entire creation became "family" for him. Nowhere is this more evident than in Francis' *Canticle of the Creatures* composed at the end of his life. It is noteworthy that Francis composed the *Canticle* while experiencing great physical and mental suffering. As Kathy Warren suggests, "his daily struggle to embrace the way of Christ in this suffering was consistent with his lifelong pursuit of walking with Christ."[17] The *Canticle* represents Francis' vision of brotherhood and sisterhood rooted in Christ. It is helpful to read the beautiful verses of the *Canticle* to appreciate its cosmic order with "Brother Sun" at its center:

> Most High, all-powerful, good Lord,
>> Yours are *the praises, the glory,* and *the honor* and *all blessing,*
> To You alone, Most High, do they belong,
>> and no human is worthy to mention Your name.
> Praised be You, my *Lord,* with all *Your creatures,*
>> especially Sir Brother Sun,
>> Who is the day and through whom You give us light.
> And he is beautiful and radiant with great splendor;
>> and bears a likeness of You, Most High One.
> *Praised* be You, my Lord, through Sister *Moon* and *the stars,*
>> in heaven You formed them clear and precious and
>> beautiful.
> Praised be You, my Lord, through Brother Wind,
>> and through the air, cloudy and serene, and every kind
>>> of weather,
>> through whom You give sustenance to Your creatures.
> *Praised* be You, my Lord, through Sister *Water,*
>> who is very useful and humble and precious and chaste.
> *Praised* be You, my Lord, through Brother *Fire,*
>> through whom *You light the night,*
>> and he is beautiful and playful and robust and strong.
> *Praised* be You, my Lord, through our Sister Mother *Earth,*
>> who sustains and governs us,
>> and who produces various *fruit* with colored flowers and
>> *herbs.*
>
> Praised be You, my Lord, through those who give pardon
>>> for Your love,
>> and bear infirmity and tribulation.
>>> Blessed are those who endure in peace
>> for by You, Most High, shall they be crowned.

. . .

> *Praise* and *bless* my *Lord* and give Him thanks
> And serve Him with great humility.[18]

Although it is not apparent to the reader, the *Canticle* is a hymn of cosmic Incarnation. The song is enclosed by the mystery of God humbly bent over in love for creation, signified by the beginning and ending words: "Most High—humility." It is "Brother Sun" who is the "day and through whom God gives us light" who is at the center of the cosmos. We might say that the Most High humbly bends down to embrace each and every element of creation in and through the Word incarnate, Jesus Christ. Everything in creation radiates the goodness of God.[19] The one who lives in Christ begins to see the world as it truly is, permeated with the divine presence. God shines through every aspect of creation. The whole world, as Angela of Foligno exclaimed, is "pregnant with God!"[20] Francis developed a deep sense of universal community because Christ became the center of his very being through the power of love. He discovered his interrelatedness to the cosmos through compassionate love by which he came to experience a unity of all things in Christ. In the *Canticle of Creatures* Francis' interior life is expressed outwardly in union with the cosmos. It is a hymn that proclaims the humanity of God as the "knot of cosmic interlacement" by which God is with all creatures in a deep sense of being intimately related to all things in creation, which are taken into his Incarnation and transformed in his glory.[21]

Kathy Warren describes the sense of creation in the *Canticle* as "reconciled space." "Creation," she writes, "is in relation as brother/sister."[22] She points out that humans do not appear in the first nine verses of the *Canticle* because they do not enjoy this harmony. They live in division. When they do appear, it is in the context of pardon and reconciliation. Humans are part of the harmony of creation only when they "pardon and bear their sufferings" since humans are weak, limited and vulnerable. To be part of the song of creation as human is to accept the human condition with its limitations and therefore to pardon, forgive and accept the suffering that is part of being human. Those who follow this path of reconciliation are freed from their blindness and can see the presence of the Most High in the simple things of creation.[23] The

Franciscan scholar Eloi Leclerc points out in the *Canticle* that Francis' movement toward the Most High and toward community are in perfect harmony. He writes: "[It is] by celebrating creatures and entering into fraternal communion with them that he [Francis] rises up to the Most High and relates himself to the One whom no human words can express."[24] This insight is similar to what Levinas indicates when he describes the trace of the transcendence in the other. Everything that exists bears an excess of goodness, a trace of the divine, so that in encountering the other as brother or sister, one encounters the source of goodness itself, the Most High God.

The humility of God means that we do not have to strain our necks looking upward or strive to climb the narrow ladder to heaven. Rather, God is bent low in love. To love each person, each creature, each element of creation as sister and brother not selfishly but for the sake of the other, to live in peace and reconciliation with all things, is to see God's goodness shining through the fragile, human nature of our lives. The face of God is hidden in the everyday ordinary person we meet along the way—the storeowner, the mechanic, the little child, the elderly woman—each in some way expresses the goodness of God. For those who know how to see, there is nothing profane here on earth. Rather, the whole creation is a sacrament of God because it is the body of Christ, that is, the body of the Word incarnate who is Jesus the risen and glorified One.

For Bonaventure, the mystery of Christ is the mystery of the Word incarnate in the diversity of creation. Bonaventure highlights the relationship of unity and plurality in the life of Francis by indicating that the more Francis entered into the mystery of Christ in his own life, the more he recognized Christ in the people and creatures around him. Francis "saw" Christ in the irreproducible uniqueness of each person and creature so that all things, each in its own way, led him to embrace Christ. Bonaventure penetrates this mystery of Christ in the world of Francis by exploring it through the lens of the overflowing goodness of God. Goodness poured out into the concrete otherness of creation is God's revelation of himself as love; thus, all of creation bears an intimate relationship with God. God is not an abstract concept for Francis but a living reality of love, and it is this love that he discovers at the heart of the Incarnation. In Bonaventure's view, one who knows Christ knows this love, and one who knows this love knows each thing of creation as the expression of this love. What Francis came to perceive in the persons he met and in the things of creation is that each person/ thing expresses the love of God and as such expresses Christ, for Christ is the love of God made visible in creation.

Although Francis' world with Christ as center attained a unity and harmony, it was not a totalizing unity of sameness but rather a unity of difference. For Bonaventure, Christ the center does not mean totalizing sameness but unified diversity, indeed, the celebration of diversity in the manifold beauty of creation. What Francis realized is that everything in creation is related to each other because everything is a "little word" of the Word of God and is therefore related to Christ. Christ is the "luminous web" of love that binds together all things in the universe. Bonaventure indicates that the fullness of the mystery of Christ is the *fullness* of otherness and difference.[25] Each person/creature expresses Christ by its own unique existence because each person/ creature is grounded in the Word of God. Each person (and creature) we might say is a "Christ center." Thus Bonaventure could write, "the center is everywhere and the circumference is nowhere," that is, Christ the center is everywhere because each center is Christ.[26] The unity of all centers in love is the fullness of the body of Christ.

The "decentered-centeredness" of Bonaventure's Christic vision with its openness to plurality and diversity, celebrates the gift of creation as the gift of God's self-communicative love. Christ is the complete center of creation, indeed, the entire universe, because Christ is the perfect expression of God as love. The radical emphasis on Incarnation throughout the life of Francis underscores the idea that God is turned toward us in love. God is not a remote, self-sufficient Being but rather God is the fecundity of goodness that seeks to share himself with another. This idea is consistent with the postmodern understanding of God. The philosopher Jean-Luc Marion claims that the name "God" does not mean "Being" but "Being as given." He writes: "the donation of God *par excellence* implies an ecstasy outside itself in which the self remains all the more itself for being in ecstasy.... God acts only to the extent that he does not remain in himself."[27]

Bonaventure contributes to a new understanding of God by transforming the remoteness of God's presence into the concrete love of neighbor and the things of creation. In Bonaventure's view, the word "God" denotes inexhaustible love in which love of the other is love of God. This love is nothing less than the humility of God's goodness shining through everything that exists, including the fragile things of creation. Bonaventure's theology impels us to rethink the meaning of Christian life in a multicultural and pluralistic world. As God is hidden in the distinct goodness of each person, so too each person images God precisely in the expression of goodness. Each person or thing that exists is a little "word" of the Word of God and as word, expresses the goodness of God. God "speaks" the Word of love—Christ—in the manifold variety of creation. When we can read the language of creation, then we know the love God has for us.

How do we discover this Christ mystery all around us? For Bonaventure, it is a matter of seeing into the depths of things, or rather seeing things as they are in relationship to God. The act of knowledge that achieves this apprehension of the Word in creation, or the creature in the Word, involves what Bonaventure calls a *contuition*. Contuition is a grasp of a perceived thing in relation to its causes, especially to its exemplary cause, the Word. This grasp is not a discursive reasoning from effect to cause. Rather it can be described as the awareness of the presence of God attained in the consciousness of a being.[28] It is not a direct vision of the Word; rather, it is a steady look at the thing in itself—but at the thing seen precisely as sign, and so in the light of its relation to the Word. The Word is known in contuition only indirectly, as that by which and in the light of which the thing can be fully known. We might think of contuition as a type of intuition, a sense of "something more" than what immediately strikes the eye. As Leonard Bowman writes, "the awareness of the Word attained through contuition requires a capacity to perceive a paradox, to hold the mind in balance so the direct object can be perceived by way of an unseen light. To see only the object is to miss its meaning; yet if it tries to see the light itself, it goes away."[29] Contuition, like contemplation, is a penetrating gaze that gets to the truth of reality.

The notion of contuition is similar to the task of the theologian who, according to Bonaventure, is to bring to light the depths of things that both reveal and veil the divine mystery.[30] Bonaventure uses the word *perscrutatio*, which means "the action of uncovering, searching out, penetrating, or fathoming," allowing the depth of the mystery to unveil itself without destroying it.[31] The theologian who is a *perscrutator* is like a treasure hunter or a seeker of pearls—she or he fathoms the unsuspected depths of the divine mystery, searches out its inmost hiding places and reveals its most beautiful jewels. Bonaventure indicates that when God expresses something of his trinitarian grandeur, it is then left to the theologian to search it out or penetrate it insofar as one allows oneself to be inhabited by the wisdom of God, which alone brings all things to light. To discover divine wisdom in this hidden order is not only to search the depth of God in himself but the depth of God hidden in his created works in which and by which he justly manifests his wisdom. This method of searching the depth of things is similar to what Jean-Luc Marion describes when he says that "depth does not indicate that 'behind' the phenomenon something else is waiting to appear, but that the very appearing of the phenomenon—as a way [of Being] and therefore as a nonbeing—reveals a depth. The depth does not dub or betray the phenomenon; it reveals it to itself."[32]

Perhaps we can interpret this "depth-seeing" of all reality by saying that we must take this world seriously, we must look deeply at each person and everything we encounter, not by looking at the surface but by looking at the details of each person, but by gazing upon every creature we encounter.[33] We often devote our attention to the outer qualities of created beings such as size, shape and color. Duns Scotus, however, called us to be aware of essential "thisness" (*haecceitas*), what makes something "this" and "not that."[34] We must see things for what they truly are in their individual creation, each uniquely loved into being by the humble love of God. Only in this way can we recognize that each human person reflects God's human face. To live in Christ is to have a heart centered in God that can penetrate the truth of things and see things in their true relationship to God. Francis became a brother to all because he saw in each person and creature the humility of God's ultimate goodness. As Francis' life indicates, the other is where we encounter God and the truth of ourselves in God. Francis' world became a global community because of Christ the center.

What does this mean, however, for those who do not know Christ? Are they not able to be part of this tremendous Christ mystery? If we deny such participation then we would have to deny that Christ is the meaning of creation and first in God's intention to love. We would have to deny that everything is ordained to Christ. Are we willing to do this? Are we willing to sacrifice the profound mystery of the Word of God for human walls of separation? Various scholars are pointing out today that other religious traditions do embody the core values of the Christ mystery without naming them as such: love, compassion, mercy, forgiveness, reconciliation, peace, enlightenment. If other religious traditions are necessary for the fullness of Christ, as Ewert Cousins suggests, then we may assume that the values of those traditions will ultimately lead to the fullness of Christ.[35] It is not important that Christ be named. It is important that Christ be lived. The healing and wholeness of humanity and the universe depends not on principles of right and wrong but on bonds of compassionate love. It is not the task of the Christian to figure out how all the parts of the Christ mystery fit together. It is important, however, to live *in* the mystery, to be fully alive in Christ. To be a Christian is not to be a member of an exclusive group nor is it to see oneself as privileged by God. Rather, it is to throw oneself into the arms of the compassionate love of God and to live a life of costly love by way of mercy, peace and reconciliation. It is, as Albert Camus wrote, to "live to the point of tears," to be passionately involved with a passionate God, to spend oneself in love by living in the Christ mystery at the heart of the universe.

Francis of Assisi desired to follow the "footprints" of Christ. A footprint is an imprint of a particular shape and size—of a particular person. How do we recognize the footprints of Christ? What do we look for? Francis saw these footprints as poverty, humility and charity: the poverty of being a created human being, the humility of our "thisness" or what makes each of us a particular person, and the charity that binds us together. These footprints eventually led him to encounter the Muslim Sultan Malek al-Kamil, to whom he desired to preach the Gospel. Traveling to Egypt during the time of the crusades, Francis was eager to accept the call of martyrdom if that meant bearing witness to Christ. Although he was caught up in the turmoil of crusades during his sojourn, he did not expect to find the Muslims so deeply God-centered with their profound reverence and respect for Allah. When Francis finally met the Sultan, he did not meet a religious adversary but a brother, for he and al-Kamil shared common ground: the centrality of God in their lives, the primacy of prayer and the conscious choice to remain "in the world" and live simple lives for the sake of God.[36] Francis discovered that, as a Christian, he was not in opposition to the Muslim leader but related to him as brother because they were united in the ultimate goodness and mercy of God. By recognizing the footprints of Christ in his sultan brother, Francis was able to transcend his religious and cultural boundaries and cross over to al-Kamil in humble love.

The life of Francis indicates to us that living in the Christ mystery does not divide but unites. If we truly see and love what we see then the walls that separate—culture from culture, religion from religion, people from people—must crumble. Where there is Christ there can be no hatred or jealousy or anger or bitterness. There can only be love, the love that unites not by clinging to things for themselves, but by giving itself away, by suffering and death for the sake of greater union. Christians who desire to be part of the Christ mystery must cast wide the nets of mercy, compassion, forgiveness, reconciliation and peace. No longer can we speak of "slave or Greek, gentile or Jew" (Galatians 3:28). Rather we must come to see that all are one in Christ Jesus. Christ is the One in the many. The Christian who lives in Christ does not try to make the other into another Christ. Rather, the one who lives in Christ realizes that in the uniqueness of the individual or creature, Christ is that other.

REFLECTION QUESTIONS

1. How do you accept people who are different from you? Are you open to them or do you avoid them?

2. Do you respect people of other religions and cultures or do you see yourself as better than others?

3. How does living in Christ help you to become a bridge to other people?

4. How can deepening your life in the humility of God help you to see the face of God in the stranger?

NOTES

[1] Hayes, "Christ, Word of God and Exemplar of Humanity," p. 6.

[2] Pirkl, "Christ, the Inspiration and Center of Life with God and Creation," p. 262.

[3] Cited in Pirkl, "Christ, the Inspiration and Center of Life with God and Creation," p. 264.

[4] Hayes, "Christ, Word of God and Exemplar of Humanity," p. 12.

[5] For an understanding of the coincidence of opposites in Bonaventure's theology see Ewert H. Cousins, *Bonaventure and the Coincidence of Opposites* (Chicago: Franciscan Herald Press, 1978).

[6] Bonaventure, *Itin.* 6.7 (V, 312). Cousins, trans. *Bonaventure*, pp. 108–109.

[7] Ewert Cousins, "Bonaventure's Christology and Contemporary Ecumenism," in *Maestro di Vita Francescana e di Sapienza Christiana*, A. Pompei, ed. vol. II (Rome: Pontificia Facoltà Teologica San Bonaventura, 1976), p. 351.

[8] Bonaventure, "The Major Legend of Saint Francis," 1.5 in *FA:ED* II, p. 534.

[9] Bonaventure, "The Major Legend of Saint Francis," 1.6 in *FA:ED* II, p. 534.

[10] Cited in Edith Wyschogrod, *Saints and Postmodernism: Revisioning Modern Philosophy* (Chicago: University of Chicago Press, 1990), p. 98.

[11] Wyschogrod, *Saints and Postmodernism*, p. 148; David Tracy, *On Naming the Present: Reflections on God, Hermeneutics, and Church* (Maryknoll, N.Y., 1994), p. 17.

[12] Tracy, *On Naming the Present*, p. 15.

[13] Bonaventure provides many examples of Francis' transformation into that which he once disdained, namely the poor and disfigured lepers. He writes, for example, "coming to a certain neighboring monastery, he asked for alms like a beggar and received it like someone unknown and despised" (see "The Major Legend of Saint Francis," 2.6 in *FA:ED* II, p. 539).

[14] Miroslav Volf, *Exclusion and Embrace: A Theological Exploration of Identity, Otherness, and Reconciliation* (Nashville: Abingdon Press, 1996), pp. 272–273.

[15] Thompson, *Jesus as Lord and Savior*, 250–271;"The Risen Christ, Transcultural Consciousness, and the Encounter of the World Religions," *Theological Studies* 37 (1976): pp. 399–405.

[16] Bonaventure, "The Major Legend of Saint Francis," 8.6 in *FA:ED* II, p. 590.

[17] Kathleen A. Warren, *Daring to Cross the Threshold: Francis of Assisi Encounters Sultan Malek al-Kamil* (Rochester, Minn.: Sisters of St. Francis, 2003), p. 98.

[18] Francis of Assisi, "The Canticle of Creatures" in *FA:ED* I, pp. 113–114.

[19] For a longer discussion on the Christ mysticism of the *Canticle* see Ilia Delio, "The Canticle of Brother Sun: A Song of Christ Mysticism," *Franciscan Studies* 52 (1992): 1–22; *A Franciscan View of Creation: Learning to Live in a Sacramental World*, vol. 2, *The Franciscan Heritage Series*, Joseph P. Chinnici, ed. (New York: The Franciscan Institute, 2003), pp. 17–20.

[20] *Angela of Foligno: Complete Works*, Paul Lachance, trans. (Mahwah, N.J.: Paulist, 1993), p. 170.

[21] Eutimio Da Arigma, *Cristo nel Cantico* (Milan: V. LePiave, 1966), p. 73.

[22] Warren, *Daring to Cross the Threshold*, p. 99.

[23] Warren, *Daring to Cross the Threshold*, p.100.

[24] Eloi Leclerc, *The Canticle of Creatures: Symbols of Union*, Matthew O'Connell, trans. (Chicago: Franciscan Herald Press, 1977), p. 208.

[25] Bonaventure, *Itin.* 5–6 (V, 308–312). See Cousins, *Bonaventure*,102–109; Ian A. MacFarland, *Difference and Identity: A Theological Anthropology* (Cleveland: Pilgrim Press, 2001), p. 57. Describing the body of Christ as the basis of difference and identity, MacFarland writes: "…the upshot of the New Testament language of the body of Christ is that the human being Jesus, though a person *in* himself, is not a person *by* himself. In other words, while the *fact* of his personhood is independent of his relationship to other beings, its *form* is not. On the contrary, because he lives out his personhood as the head of a body that incorporates an indeterminate number of human persons, his identity as a human person is inseparable from his relationship with all these other persons."

[26] Bonaventure, *Itin.* 5.8 (V, 310). Cousins, trans. *Bonaventure*, p. 100.

[27] Jean-Luc Marion, "Metaphysics and Phenomenology: A Summary for Theologians," in *The Postmodern God: A Theology Reader*, Graham Ward, ed. (Malden, Mass: Blackwell Publishers, 1997), p. 292.

[28] For a definition of *contuition* see Delio, *Simply Bonaventure*, p. 199.

[29] Leonard J. Bowman, "Bonaventure's 'Contuition' and Heidegger's 'Thinking': Some Parallels," *Franciscan Studies* 37 (1977): 24–25.

[30] Emmanuel Falque, "The Phenomenological Act of *Perscrutatio* in the Proemium of St. Bonaventure's Commentary on the Sentences," Elisa Mangina, trans. *Medieval Philosophy and Theology* 10 (2001): 6.

[31] Falque, "The Phenomenological Act of *Perscrutati*" p. 9.

[32] Jean-Luc Marion, *Reduction et donation: Recherches sur Husserl, Heidegger, et la phénomenologie* (Paris: Presses Universitaires de France, 1989), p. 63.

[33] For an understanding of gazing in this context see my book *Franciscan Prayer* (Cincinnati: St. Anthony Messenger Press, 2004).

[34] Mary Beth Ingham, *Scotus for Dunces: An Introduction to the Subtle Doctor* (New York: The Franciscan Institute, 2003), pp. 52–55.

[35] Ewert Cousins's work on Bonaventure and world religions has set the foundation for exploring the fullness of Christ in light of diversity and religious pluralism. See Ewert Cousins, "The Trinity and World Religions," *Journal of Ecumenical Studies* 7.3 (Summer 1970): 476–498; "Bonaventure and World Religions," in *S. Bonaventura 1274–1974*, vol. III (Grottaferrata: Collegio S. Bonaventura, 1973), pp. 696–706. See also his chapter on "The Fullness of the Mystery of Christ" in *Christ of the 21st Century* (Rockport, Mass.: Element Books, 1992), pp.163–193.

[36] Warren, *Daring to Cross the Threshold*, pp. 48–49.

Chapter Seven

CHRISTIC CHRISTIANS

*To live in an evolutionary spirit means
to engage with full ambition and without
any reserve in the structure of the present,
and yet to let go and flow into a new
structure when the right time has come.*
—Eric Jantsch

I n the year I was born, one of the greatest mystics of the twentieth century died of a sudden stroke on Easter Sunday in upstate New York and was buried in a small plot of land that is now part of the Culinary Institute of America. The Jesuit scientist Pierre Teilhard de Chardin had such profound insight to the evolution of the universe in Christ that, to this day, the depths of his insight are still obscure, although much work has been done to interpret his ideas. His writings on Christ and evolution were banned during his lifetime and he lived much of his life on the edge of exile because no one understood the meaning of his universe. As a paleontologist, Teilhard was aware of an evolutionary creation. His own scientific work uncovered some of the earliest human prototypes, including the spurious Piltdown man.[1] His deep Christian faith coupled with his love of science led him to a unique love of the material world, which he saw imbued with divine meaning. He summed up his vision of faith by saying: "I believe that the universe is in evolution, I believe that evolution proceeds toward spirit, I believe that spirit is fully realized in a form of personality, I believe that the supremely personal is the universal Christ."[2]

For Teilhard, Christ is the goal and center of the universe and the reason for the evolution of the universe itself. As the goal of the universe, Christ is the Omega point, drawing all things to their fulfillment. Through his penetrating view of the universe, Teilhard found Christ present in the entire cosmos, from the least particle of matter to the convergent human community. The world, he claimed, is like a crystal lamp illumined from within by the light of Christ. For those who can see, Christ shines in this diaphanous universe, through the cosmos and in matter.[3] The whole process of evolution, according to Teilhard, is a movement toward greater interiorization and complexity, from simple isolated structures to complex unions, from matter to spirit. He called this evolution in Christ a "Christogenesis." The whole evolutionary universe is a "coming-to-be" of Christ.[4] Teilhard's writings were banned by the religious authorities of the Catholic church because they reflected a type of Christian pantheism, which was incorrectly interpreted by some as a "fatal naturalism."[5] Yet, what Teilhard grasped was no different from the insight of Francis of Assisi or Bonaventure, namely, Incarnation is what creation is all about. In the Incarnation, God humbly bends down to lift created human nature into unity with divine nature. What Teilhard realized is that, in an evolutionary universe, God continues to bend low in love because the fullness of the Incarnation has not yet come to be.

Teilhard's Christogenic universe invites us to broaden our understanding of Christ; not to abandon what we profess or proclaim in word and practice but to allow these beliefs to open us up to a world of evolution of which we are vital members. One way to help us expand our understanding of Christ is through the idea of "axial consciousness." In his book *Christ of the 21st Century*, Ewert Cousins described an "axial shift" in consciousness. The basis of Cousins's idea is the work of the German philosopher Karl Jaspers who noted that between 800 and 200 B.C. a transformation of consciousness occurred around the earth in three geographical regions: China, India and the West, which eventually became polarized as Orient and Occident. From these three regions the great civilizations of Asia, the Middle East and Europe developed. Because this transformation affected all aspects of culture, including consciousness itself, Jaspers referred to it as an axial period since "it gave birth to everything which since then, the human person has been able to be."[6] Unlike the pre-axial period, which was marked by a tribal consciousness, that is, a deep sense of the collective community or tribe, nurtured by myth and ritual, as well as a sense of relatedness to the cosmos, the first axial period was marked by individual consciousness. "Know thyself" became the watchword of Greece. The *Upanishad* (Hindu treatise) identified the *atman*, the transcendent center of the self. The Buddha charted the way of individual enlightenment; the Jewish prophets awakened individual moral responsibility.

The emergence of axial consciousness, marked by a sense of individual identity, self-transcendence, autonomy and freedom, gave rise to the world religions: Hinduism, Buddhism, Taoism, Confucianism, Judaism followed by Christianity and Islam. The sense of individual identity, according to Cousins, is the most characteristic mark of the first axial consciousness.[7] Nowhere is the mark of individual consciousness more apparent than in the religious quest. While the Greek philosopher Plotinus described the human journey as a flight of the "alone to the Alone," Christians translated this idea into the monastic quest for union with the divine. One of the most distinctive forms of spirituality that emerged in the first axial period was monasticism, the solitary search for the divine ground of being, that is, for God. Monasticism did not exist among pre-axial (primal) peoples, Cousins states, because primal consciousness did not contain the distinct center of individuality necessary to produce the monk as a religious type.[8]

If we turn our attention to the twenty-first century, we can discern another transformation of consciousness, which Cousins refers to as the second axial period. Like the first axis, it is happening simultaneously around the earth and will shape the horizon of consciousness for future centuries. Second axial period consciousness is characterized by global consciousness. Through the progress of technology and mass media, people are becoming more aware of belonging to humanity as a whole and not to a specific group. For the first time since the appearance of human life on our planet, Cousins writes, all of the tribes, all of the nations, all of the religions are beginning to share a common history.[9]

This new global consciousness must be seen from two perspectives: 1) from a horizontal perspective, cultures and religions must meet each other on the surface of the globe, entering into creative encounters that will produce a *complexified collective consciousness*. Cousins borrows the term "complexified collective consciousness" from Teilhard to describe the convergence of centers of consciousness in the evolutionary process.[10] 2) From a vertical perspective, cultures and religions must plunge their roots deep into the earth in order to provide a stable and secure base for future development. This new global consciousness must be organically ecological, supported by structures that will ensure justice and peace. What Cousins indicates is that the second axial period is communal, global, ecological and cosmic. It is not merely a shift from first axial period consciousness. It is an advancement in the whole evolutionary process.

You may be wondering how axial period consciousness relates to the humility of God. While we have been exploring the humility of God up to now by way of Franciscan theology (developed in the first axial period), the notion of Christ as the center and goal of creation is more congruent to second axial period consciousness than to first axial period consciousness. It seems to me that our Christian theology today is not only caught between the cracks of modernity and postmodernity—between rationalism and relativism—it is caught between the gap of first and second axial period consciousness.[11] Our world today is a pluralism of cultures, religions, races, languages and practices. It is not as if new cultures or world religions only recently emerged. It is rather that we have become consciously aware of this plurality through technology, travel and a global economy. Switch on a television screen and you can stand in a Kurdish desert, the city of Baghdad, or amidst the rubble of a demolished home in Afghanistan. Step outside your door and you can eat Indian, Mexican, Italian or Ethiopian cuisine. Go to the bank and you may find a woman in African dress or covered with a burka or a man with a turban or yarmulke. We are becoming increasingly aware that the world is, indeed, a global village. Our neighbors are no longer Protestant or fallen-away Catholics. They are Hindu, Coptic Orthodox, Jewish and Buddhist with a variety of religious rituals and beliefs. This new age of consciousness is both a blessing and a curse: a blessing insofar as we see that the human family is delightfully rich in diversity and shares a common human desire for love and peace. It is a curse because we Christians find it difficult to live in a global age of diversity with an exclusive Christology that was developed in a hierarchically static world of first axial period consciousness. We are divided between a medieval theology, postmodern culture and a globalized world. The question for Christians today is no longer "are you saved?" but "what does it mean to be saved?" Who is saved? What are we saved from in a fifteen-billion-year-old universe? We utter prayers of Christian belief but the content is wearing thin because when we step outside our door and meet a stranger we are increasingly unsure of the meaning of Christ. Does Jesus save only the billion Catholics of the world to the exclusion of the billions of Earth's peoples? How can we proclaim that the earth itself will be saved and not Muslims or Hindus? What kind of God is this who is incarnate anyway?

The last question is the easiest to answer because it is the theme of this book. The kind of God who is incarnate is a God of humble love, a God who has loved everything into being and who bends over in love to sustain every being. This is not a God who is remote and removed from creation. This is a God who is faithful in love, a God of involved goodness, a God who so loves the world that he gives the world freedom to be itself. This God of faithful love is Trinity, a God of relationships. God bends down in love for creation not in spite of Jesus Christ but because of Christ: the Father loves the Son in the Spirit. We are caught up in the mystery of the Word made flesh because we are caught up in the Father's eternal love for the Son. As we have mentioned before (and trying to drive home the point): Christ does not belong to us, we belong to Christ. Christ is the meaning of what the universe and we are about. This is not a new idea (it is rooted in the New Testament) but it takes on new meaning in the second axial period. Teilhard de Chardin understood this Christ mystery at the heart of the universe in a deep and profound way and realized that the mystery includes, in a particular way, every person who bears the name "Christian." Yes, the universe is in evolution toward the fullness of Christ but it is the task of Christians to help personalize the universe in the love of Christ. We are called to be co-creators of the universe, to "christify" the universe by our actions of love.[12] This is not to say that peoples of other religions cannot christify the universe through love—they can. It is to say, however, that this is the distinct Christian vocation—to discover Christ at the heart of the universe in all peoples, cultures, religions and tribes; to discover the earth as the body of Christ.

In Bonaventure's view, everything finds meaning in relation to the Word of God because everything is created through the Word (John 1:4). When the Word became flesh the truth of reality was disclosed. Those who know Christ know the light of the world and thus are to act according to the light. But do we? If we truly believed that Christ is the center of our life and world, that each of us is a member of the body of Christ, and that body is incomplete without us, that the fullness of Christ encompasses all peoples, all races, religions and cultures, indeed, the entire universe, would we harm our neighbor? Injure or abuse the earth? Kill our enemies? Ignore the poor, the homeless or the outcasts of our society? Pursue wealth, power and control? If we truly believed that all is Christ, would we continue to crucify Christ? Or would we act according to the law of Jesus: love, mercy and compassion? Would we be willing to lay down our lives out of love for the sake of the other? If we truly believed that Christ is center of the universe, would we be so private about the good news we hold so sacred?

Teilhard called Christians to participate in the process of Christogenesis, for the entire creation is waiting to give birth to God's promise—the fullness of love (Romans 8:19–20). Sin, we might say, is the unwillingness or inability to participate in the coming to fullness of all things in Christ. It is everything that stands in our path of relationship to God. In Teilhard's view, a Christ whose features do not adapt themselves to the requirements of a world that is evolutive in structure will tend more and more to be eliminated out of hand. When we comply with the erasure of Christ from the world because we fail to live in the mystery, this too is sin. Teilhard asked Christians to "christify" the world by our actions, by immersing ourselves in the world, plunging our hands we might say into the soil of the earth and touching the roots of life This is radically different from Christian writers of the early church who emphasized that we are "pilgrims and strangers" in this world, passing through it like a ship on a stormy sea. Even today we find some who believe that the perfection of Christian life is to be sought in a "flight from the world" because the world, the flesh and the devil are temptations in the pursuit of God. Only by avoiding the world and its temptations can we find God.

The fact of the matter is, however, that the universe is our home and like every home we must live in it. If we ask, why be involved in a messy world that is often an obstacle to finding God? The answer is simply that God is involved in the mess. When we search for a clean-cut, uninvolved God of power and control high up in the starry heavens we can be sure that we have abandoned a God who is humbly bent down in love for a fragile and finite creation. "God loved the world so much that he gave his only Son" (John 3:16). God did not send the Son merely to repair the damage due to sin. God sent the Son because God loves the Son and would have sent the Son even if humans never sinned because the lover has from all eternity sought a beloved. Christ is the primary lover of the infinite love of God. And here is the mystery as Bonaventure and Teilhard grasped it. The mystery of Christ and our lives as humans are intertwined. We are caught up in the eternal love of the Father for the Son, that is, we are caught up in the Spirit of love. Without us humans (and all creation) Christ does not exist. Without a living Christ, Christianity becomes a system of doctrines and beliefs, a dead letter, not a living Word of God. "If Christ has not been raised [from the dead] then our preaching is useless and your believing it is useless," Paul writes (1 Corinthians 15:14). The witness to the living Christ is the human proclamation, "we have seen the Lord!"

If the humility of God is really all about Incarnation, then we must admit that the humility of God involves our lives as well because we are members of the Body of Christ. The fullness of the Incarnation depends on us—our actions, our lives, our willingness to be Christ in the world, to see Christ in the world, to "christify" the world. The humility of God must shine through our lives if the evolution of the universe is to progress toward its completion in Christ. God must bend down in love *in us* and we must bend down in love for one another. Without our witness to the humility of God's love, Christ is not raised from the dead and our preaching the "good news" is useless. The Christian today must bear witness to the living Christ—all peoples, all cultures, all religions and the entire earth—through a spirit of selfless, compassionate love. Christianity is a religion of the future, as Teilhard proclaimed, and Christians must lead the universe into the future by seeking the unity of all things in love, the luminous web of love that is the body of Christ. As Hayes writes, "we are not to become carbon copies of this historical Jesus nor of Francis nor of anyone else. We are to fill the Christ-form with the elements of our own personal life and thus embody something of the Word in ourselves in a distinctive and personal way."[13] I believe this is what it means to follow Christ in an evolutionary world and to be part of the evolution in Christ, as the universe itself moves toward the Omega point. Each of us has a distinct role in the Christ mystery and the fullness of the mystery of Christ is either enhanced or diminished by the degree of our participation. Christ comes to be the fullness of the universe when we become the fullness of Christ.

Christian life in the second axial period demands a renewed sense of life in the universe. This new life includes belief in the centrality of Christ as the web of relationship, the primacy of compassionate love and the celebration of difference. To believe in Christ the center is to believe that the "center is everywhere," first within the human soul, then in every person and creature, and then in every element of the universe—every center is a Christ center. It is the Spirit of love that binds together all the centers into the one Body of Christ. Living in Christ the center means that we must see the world with contemplative vision and find a space within us to embrace the stranger, the widow and the orphan. Contemplation is a penetrating gaze that gets to the heart of reality.[14] It is looking into the depths of things with the eyes of the heart and seeing them in their true relation to God. It is a type of vision that sees things for their true worth, their individual uniqueness and distinction, the fact that each thing is singularly wanted and loved by God. Francis of Assisi was a "contuitive person" who contemplated God in all of creation. "In beautiful things," Bonaventure wrote, "he

[Francis] contuited Beauty itself / out of them all making for himself to lay hold of a *ladder* / through which he could climb up him / *who is utterly desirable*."[15] What we see and the way we see must cause us to act in a new way. Spiritual vision creates brotherhood and sisterhood because as we see, so we love. We recognize that we are integrally related to one another because we are integrally related to God. Contemplative vision leads us to see the goodness of God in the other and to bind ourselves to the other in compassionate love. Contemplation is essential to Christian life in a Christic universe.

If we reduce Christ merely to a personal Savior and confine Christ to an institutional church we can be sure that the meaning of Christ will become increasingly irrelevant in a complex world of cultural and religious diversity. Neither Christianity nor salvation itself is a private, individual matter. Salvation, Thomas Merton wrote, means rescuing the person from the individual or, we might say, it is bringing the individual into personhood through an experience of love.[16] To be a human person alive in God is based not on *what* we are or what we do but *who* we are in relation to God, self, others and world. It means to be in relationship with another by which the other sounds through in one's life. Living in Christ is to rescue us from the gravity of our individual isolated egos and transform us into relational beings, in the image of God. Francis of Assisi became a person because he allowed the God of humble love to breathe through his life and in the lives of others he met along the way. The acme of our originality, Teilhard de Chardin wrote, is not in our individuality but in being a person.[17] And the only way to become fully personal is through union with others since the basis of union is the irreproducible core of self: union differentiates.[18]

How do we strive for this transformation in Christ, this salvation from rampant individualism to relational personhood? One of the most significant lessons of the life of Francis is the value of poverty—not material poverty but the poverty of being, the poverty that recognizes everything we have is gift, the poverty of being created by God. Poverty, for Francis, is related to love. In his view, we fail in love because we live in the spirit of possessiveness and self-appropriation, grabbing for ourselves what belongs to others. He advised his followers to live *sine proprio*—not without things but without possessing things, for when we possess things we think that we do not need other people or have a responsibility of love toward them. Francis had profound insight to the human person and he placed poverty in the context of human relationships. Three areas where he speaks of living *sine proprio* are: 1) our inner selves and what we possess for ourselves; 2) our relationships with others and what we possess in relation to others; and 3) our relationship to God and what we possess in relation to God.[19] In all three areas Francis asked of his followers to "hold back nothing of yourselves for yourselves, / so that He Who gives Himself totally to you / may receive you totally."[20] Only relationships of poverty and humility, in Francis' view, can undo the injustices of the self-centered person. Only when we are dependent on another can we renounce autonomy, power and control, and accept the gift of the other in whom God lives. But to really live poverty we must ask, how much are we willing to let go? Can we accept God's goodness in our neighbor who is different from us? Poverty, therefore, relates to our humanity; material poverty is only sacramental of the deeper poverty of being human. Material dispossession should lead to a poverty of interdependency, to accepting goodness from the other, and accepting the other as the goodness of God. Only care for another truly humanizes life.

The value of poverty, as it helps form the Christic person, relates to our capacity for compassionate love, to love the stranger and the one who is different from us. The truly poor person has space within his or her heart to let the stranger in. In his book *Exclusion and Embrace*, Miroslav Volf describes a "phenomenology of embrace" that may help us understand the meaning of poverty here. An embrace, Volf writes, begins with opening the arms. "Open arms are a gesture of the body reaching for the other. They are a sign of discontent with my own self-enclosed identity, a code of *desire* for the other. I do not want to be myself only; I want the other to be part of who I am and I want to be part of the other."[21] Open arms therefore signify that I have "*created space* in myself for the other to come in and that I have made a movement out of myself so as to enter the space created by the other."[22] A self that is "full of itself" can neither receive the other nor make genuine movement toward the other.[23] Thus open arms signify an opening in the self for the other to enter and a gesture of invitation to the other that they are welcome to come in.[24] In this respect, a phenomenology of embrace relates to dialogue. Dialogue, Leonard Swidler states, is a conversation with those who think differently, the primary purpose of which is for me to learn from the other.[25] It is a crossing over the threshold of difference into the other to be with the other and to allow the other to cross over into one's life. Dialogue is transcending the boundaries of difference in pursuit of creative union and this is possible only when we are capable of embrace.

Compassionate love not only requires space in the human heart for the stranger but it requires a capacity to suffer with another. Francis of Assisi discovered a healing love in the wounds of the crucified Christ and it was through his receptivity to grace that he learned to love by way of compassion. Compassion, as scientists tell us today, has a real biological basis. There are neurons in the brain that mirror another person's emotional experience so that we really do "feel" what the other person is experiencing.[26] How do we learn to "feel" for others in such a way that their sorrow becomes our sorrow and their joy our joy? Bonaventure claims that we learn compassion by meditating on the mystery of Christ crucified where we can see God's overflowing love for us to the point of suffering and death. Our problem, he states, is that we have hardened hearts—as hard as rocks. We can look on the Crucified and be neither "struck with terror nor moved with compassion."[27] I wonder today if we have so overly domesticated the cross that we not only ignore its scandalous image but we relate to it as an art object, expensive to buy and beautiful to look at. We need to sit before the cross and ponder our own lives in this awesome mystery of suffering and love. We need to rediscover the cross as the mirror of compassion, the place where we can see ourselves for what we truly are and where we can learn to love by way of suffering in, with and for another. We need a renewed mysticism of the cross as our pathway into the fullness of Christ.

To live in the mysticism of the cross is to live a eucharistic life. To live in the Eucharist is to live in the Body of Christ—the body that refuses to keep bodies separate but unites them through suffering love. It is to live in the spirit of crucified love. Volf states that following the Crucified does not mean moving from the particularity of the body to the universality of the Spirit but from separated bodies to the community of interrelated bodies—the one body in the Spirit with many discrete members.[28] The Body of Christ lives as a complex interplay of differentiated bodies. It is the Spirit that breaks through the self-enclosed worlds we inhabit, recreates us and sets us on a road toward new creation. "A catholic personality is a personality enriched by otherness," Volf writes. The Spirit unlatches the door of one's heart saying, "You are not only you; others belong to you too."[29] A catholic personality, therefore, requires a catholic community. Each one must say, "I am not only I; all others belong to me too." The heart of the Christian life, centered in the cross, involves creating space in oneself for the other to come in. According to Volf, when God sets out to embrace the enemy, the result is the cross. On the cross the dancing circle of self-giving and mutually indwelling Trinitarian persons of love opens up for the enemy. We are embraced by the divine persons who love us with the same love with which they love each other and therefore make space for us within their own eternal embrace.[30] Just as the arms of the crucified Christ are a sign of a space in God's self and an invitation for the enemy to come in, so too we are to do the same.[31]

Eucharist is ritual time in which we celebrate this divine "making space for us and inviting us in." What happens to us must be done by us. Having been embraced by God, we must make space for others in ourselves and invite them in—even our enemies.[32] In receiving Christ's broken body and blood we, in a sense, receive all those whom Christ received by suffering. The other of embrace is not just the brother or sister inside the self-enclosed ecclesial community. The other is also the enemy outside us. All are taken into the embrace by being forgiven and called "brother" and "sister." We who have been embraced by the outstretched arms of the crucified God open our arms even for our enemies, to make space in ourselves for them and to invite them in, so that together we may rejoice in the eternal embrace of the triune God.[33]

Francis' life was eucharistic because his was the body of Christ given over to others in a spirit of forgiveness and reconciliation, for the sake of healing, wholeness and peace. Beatrice Bruteau writes that "the essence of forgiveness...is not a statement about the past. It is an act of making the future....the energetic radiation of a good will for the sake of the future."[34] Crucified love is love that creates a new future because it is the love that makes space for the other to enter in and share life. This is the love of salvation because it is the love of healing that restores persons to unity and peace. It is the love of community because it recognizes that the wholeness of community requires healing in the midst of wounded, broken bodies. A person can live in the spirit of crucified love only when she or he *believes* that they are loved. "The root of Christian love," Merton wrote, "is not the will to love, but *the faith that one is loved*."[35] To live in the spirit of crucified Christ is to live in the trust of God's fidelity, God's "I love you, I am with you," in the human heart. This faithful love of God empowers us to give birth to Christ. It makes us free to face our enemies and those who hate us because it makes us free to see the goodness of God in the mirror of wounded bodies and souls—those whom we would otherwise reject, as Francis first rejected the leper. To love in the spirit of crucified love, to let this love be shown in the "birthing" of Christ, is to create a new future of life, a future of healing wounds, divisions, hatred and animosity, the healing that brings peace. Bruteau writes: "If we really accept that creation is always new, and if we ourselves are active participants in this new creating, then we are always facing the future."[36] If we desire a future of unity and peace then we must participate in the path of salvation that brings together that which is divided. Christ crucified is the way to peace through the unity of love.

Francis' life was not simply waiting for God to do good things for him. Rather, he actively pursued God by becoming a lover of Christ. Relationship is a mutuality of desires—our desire for God and God's desire for us. Francis strove to love Christ wholeheartedly through poverty and humility to the extent that, at the end of his life, he looked like Christ. We become what we love and the way we love shapes the world around us. Francis' world became "Christic" because Christ became the center of his life. Through his compassionate love, the world around him was healed and made whole because compassionate love shaped him into a vessel of peace.

Like Francis, we too *are* the Body of Christ, each of us with our own bodies and spirits, minds and hearts. Each of us is called to "re-present" Christ because each of us is created through the Word and is a little word incarnate, which longs to express itself through the Spirit of love. The universe yearns for its completion in God but cannot attain it apart from us. As we move forward in this new age of consciousness, we are called to be aware of our self-transcendent desire for union in love—to christify the universe. We are Christian because we believe that we and all creation find meaning and purpose in Christ. But until we allow this mystery of Christ to touch us, embrace us and change us, we remain outside the mystery. Christ remains distant to us, as if Christ were an individual different from us in the same way that our neighbors are different from us. But Christ is not outside us; rather, Christ lives in us. We are Christ, members of Christ's body through the Spirit. In his last conference in Bangkok, Thomas Merton sought to explore the Christ mystery in a global context, saying, "What we are asked to do at present is not so much to speak of Christ as to let him live in us so that people may find him by feeling how he lives in us."[37]

Prayer leads us into the mystery of Christ by opening us up to this mystery in our lives. To become a "Christic" person is to come to a new level of personhood, a transcendent level, by which we realize that the God whose goodness permeates our lives also lives in our brothers and sisters. Therefore, we humans are not like separate atoms in the universe. Rather the goodness of God in me is also in my neighbor; thus I am incomplete apart from my neighbor who is my brother and sister. If I am to find God then I must gaze on my neighbor who is a mirror of Christ. If I am to come to the fullness of who I am I must love my neighbor in whom I dwell and who is something of me. To come to this new level of personhood is to contemplate Christ, to penetrate the truth of the Christ mystery in the community of humankind. Beatrice Bruteau, describes the mystery of Christ for our time in a way that echoes the thought of Bonaventure. She writes:

To enter by our transcendent freedom into Christ and to become a New Creation means to enter by faith into the future of every person and into the very heart of creativity itself, into the future of God.

To be "in Christ" is to accept the offer that Jesus makes, to be food for his friends....One must renounce the lordship pattern of organizing social relations. One must forsake being either dominant or submissive. One must undergo this...particular mutation in consciousness. To be "in Christ" is to enter into the revolutionary events of Holy Thursday by...letting an old modality of consciousness die and seeing a new one rise to life.

To be "in Christ" is to abandon thinking of oneself only in terms of categories and abstractions by which one may be externally related to others and to coincide with oneself as a transcendent center of energy that lives in God and in one's fellows—because that is where the Christ lives, in God and in us.

To be "in Christ" is to experience oneself as an initiative of free energy radiating out to give life abundantly to all, for that is the function of the Christ. To be "in Christ" is to be an indispensable member of a living body, which is the Body of Christ. To be "in Christ" is to be identified with the Living One who is not to be sought among the dead, for the Living One is the One who is Coming to Be.

If I am asked then, "Who do you say I am?" my answer is: "You are the new and ever renewing act of creation. You are all of us, as we are united in You. You are all of us as we live in one another. You are all of us in the whole cosmos as we join in Your exuberant act of creation. You are the Living One who improvises at the frontier of the future; and it has not yet appeared what You shall be."[38]

What Bruteau highlights is that living in a cosmic Christic world is a matter of living in the mystery of Christ. This mystery includes us humans as co-creators of an evolutionary universe. It is in the mystery of the human person that the fulfillment of the universe lies. Love has the power to transform, and the power of transforming love lies within us, for each of us has the power to make present the living God. I wonder, however, if we have not become too privatized in our culture and too sedentary in our ways to really live the Christ mystery in its fullness today and to go forward in newness, spontaneity and freedom. We have something of the middle-class blues and these blues bear the weight of inertia. Living in the fullness of the mystery of Christ is to believe that every person regardless of race, religion or creed, belongs to Christ, and that loving our neighbor in Christ is the path to unity in God. Such unity extends not only to our brothers and sisters of other cultures, religions and languages but to the earth itself, recognizing that the earth and we are on the journey to God together.

Bonaventure calls us to contemplate the goodness of God in our world. Too often we search for God in all the wrong places—we seek a God of power and control. But the humility of God is such that God dwells in the brokenness of our own lives and in the broken lives of others. Living in relation to a humble God should cause us to look more deeply at concrete reality because that is where the goodness of God is hidden. To see this goodness must lead to solidarity with all creation because when we recognize the primordial mystery of love as the source of the other as well as our ourselves, we find a common ground and can unite ourselves to the other in love. Solidarity with all people and solidarity with the earth are signs of those living in relation to the cosmic Christ, the Living One. The key to solidarity is finding Christ at the center of our lives so that we may recognize Christ as the center of other lives, indeed, as the center of the world. This solidarity means bonds of real relationship, sharing with the other in such a way that we are open and receptive to the gift of the other, loving others by way of compassion. The justice and peace that we long for in our world must be a justice and peace of the earth, a justice of relationship with the natural elements, with ecosystems and rain forests, with all creatures of creation. For in the end (whatever that end will be) the earth will not be annihilated or destroyed but together with humanity will be transformed in the love of God. There will be a new heaven and earth with Christ as center, a center of love, happiness and peace. For Bonaventure, Christ is the center of our life in God but this center is crucified and glorified because suffering and death mark the passage into God. We must descend with Christ into the darkness of our humanity—the suffering, the death, the horror of destruction that so violates human reason—that we may rise anew with Christ in the unity of love. In a world marked by violence and death, suffering does not have the last word. The last word is love and that love is the fullness of the Living One, the Christ, who is the Word of God.

REFLECTION QUESTIONS

1. We are in the process of being made into Christ—*Christification*. Such assimilation is not "cloning" but union with Christ. How do you understand your assimilation into Christ in light of your own unique identity?
2. What is the "universal call to holiness" as a Christic vocation?
3. The world, according to Teilhard, is worth "throwing ourselves into." This opposes a spirituality which rejects the world. Where do you stand with regard to the world and your life in Christ?
4. How do you understand Paul's admonition that in Christ "there is neither male nor female, Jew or Greek, slave or free" but all have been made one in Christ?

NOTES

[1] In the early part of the twentieth century, fossil remains of an ancient Pleistocene hominid were found in the Piltdown quarries in Sussex, England. These fossils were believed to belong to a hominid type, the "Piltdown man," that formed the "missing link" between apes and humans. However, the discovery was later revealed to be a hoax. Stephen Jay Gould, a paleontologist at Harvard University, claimed that Teilhard was involved in the Piltdown hoax. See Stephen Jay Gould, *The Panda's Thumb: More Reflections in Natural History* (New York: W.W. Norton and Company, 1980).

[2] Cited in De Lubac, *Teilhard de Chardin: The Man and His Meaning*, p. 169, n. 1.

[3] This is the thesis of Teilhard's classic *The Divine Milieu*. See also his "My Universe," in *Process Theology*, Ewert H. Cousins, ed. (New York: Newman Press, 1971), pp. 249–255.

[4] Pierre Teilhard de Chardin, *The Phenomenon of Man*, Bernard Wall, trans. (New York: Harper and Row, 1959), pp. 297–298.

[5] De Lubac, *Teilhard de Chardin: The Man and His Meaning*, p. 186.

[6] Karl Jaspers, *The Origin and Goal of History*, Michael Bullock, trans. (New Haven, Conn.: Yale University Press, 1953), pp. 1, 23, 27.

[7] Ewert H. Cousins, *Christ of the 21st Century* (Rockport, Mass.: Element Books, 1992), pp. 2–4.

[8] Cousins, *Christ of the 21st Century*, p. 7.

[9] Cousins, *Christ of the 21st Century*, p. 7–10.

[10] See Pierre Teilhard de Chardin, *Activation of Energy*, Rene Hague, trans. (New York: Harcourt Brace Jovanovich, 1970), pp. 30–31, 101–103.

[11] For more appropriate distinctions between modernity and postmodernity see Stanley Grenz, *A Primer on Postmodernism* (Grand Rapids, Mich.: William B. Eerdmans, 1995); *Franciscan Identity and Postmodern Culture*, Kathleen A. Warren, ed. (New York: The Franciscan Institute, 2002).

[12] The idea of the Christian vocation as "Christifying matter" was Teilhard's passion. Only in this way, he realized, can the new heaven and earth that we long for be attained. He also realized, however, that traditional theology prevents the Christian from being passionately involved in the world. See Christopher F. Mooney, "Teilhard de Chardin and Christian Spirituality," in *Process Theology*, pp. 308–315.

[13] Hayes, "Christ, the Word and Exemplar of Humanity," p. 15.

[14] Michael W. Blastic, *Spirit and Life: A Journal of Contemporary Franciscanism* "Contemplation and Compassion: A Franciscan Ministerial Spirituality," Anthony Carrozzo, Kenneth Himes and Vincent Cushing, eds. (New York: The Franciscan Institute, 1997), p. 168.

[15] Bonaventure, "The Major Legend of Saint Francis," 9.1 in *FA:ED* II, p. 596.

[16] Merton, *New Seeds of Contemplation*, p. 38.

[17] Teilhard de Chardin, *Phenomenon of Man*, p. 263.

[18] Teilhard de Chardin, *Phenomenon of Man*, p. 262.

[19] For a good discussion on Francis and poverty see Regis J. Armstrong, *Saint Francis of Assisi* (New York: Crossroad, 1994), pp. 154–165.

[20] Francis of Assisi, "A Letter to the Entire Order," 29 in *FA:ED* I, p. 118.

[21] Volf, *Exclusion and Embrace*, p. 141.

[22] Volf, *Exclusion and Embrace*, p. 142.

[23] Volf, *Exclusion and Embrace*, p. 141.

[24] For an explanation of embrace and not-understanding see Volf, *Exclusion and Embrace*, pp. 145–156.

[25] Leonard Swidler, "The Age of Global Dialogue," in *Doors of Understanding: Conversations on Global Spirituality in Honor of Ewert Cousins*, Steven L. Chase, ed. (Quincy, Ill.: Franciscan Press, 1998), pp. 19–20.

[26] Heather Wax, "See Me, Feel Me: The Twists of Empathy," *Science and Theology News* 4.6 (February 2004): 40.

[27] Bonaventure, *Lig. vit.* 29 (VIII, 79). Cousins, trans. *Bonaventure*, p. 154.

[28] Volf, *Exclusion and Embrace*, p. 48.

[29] Volf, *Exclusion and Embrace*, p. 51.

[30] Volf, *Exclusion and Embrace*, p. 129.

[31] Volf, *Exclusion and Embrace*, p. 128.

[32] Volf, *Exclusion and Embrace*, p. 128.

[33] Volf, *Exclusion and Embrace*, p. 131.

[34] Beatrice Bruteau, *The Grand Option: Personal Transformation and a New Creation* (Notre Dame, Ind.: University of Notre Dame Press, 2001), p. 129.

[35] Merton, *New Seeds of Contemplation*, p. 75.

[36] Bruteau, *Grand Option*, p. 171.

[37] Thomas Merton, quoted in James Forest, *Living With Wisdom: A Life of Thomas Merton* (Maryknoll, N.Y.: Orbis Books, 1991), p. 216.

[38] Bruteau, *Grand Option*, pp. 172–173.

Chapter Eight

DIVINIZATION

Our discovery of God is, in a way, God's discovery of us. We cannot go to heaven to find Him because we have no way of knowing where heaven is or what it is. He comes down from heaven and finds us...
—Thomas Merton, *New Seeds of Contemplation*

We may wonder why the humility of God leads us to a Christic vocation in the universe, but hopefully by now the answer is somewhat (ever so slightly?) evident. If it is not then we would have to admit that we are so entrenched in a religion of doctrine, rituals and obligations that we are completely unaware of the fact that to live in the humility of God is to live in Christ, and to live in Christ is to be in relation to a living Person. Christ is the Living Person at the center of the universe and our lives in Christ are meant to participate in the completion of the Body of Christ. Teilhard de Chardin once said that the problem with Christianity is that it makes its followers inhuman. By this radical statement he meant that Christianity isolates people instead of merging them with the mass, it causes them to lose interest in the common task, and it does not make people aware of their divine responsibilities, to divinize the world. True. Who gets up in the morning wondering how they are going to divinize the world that day? How many Christians even know what "divinization" is? That to be "divinized" is to become "like God," to participate in the infinite goodness of God? Yes, we are called to divinize the world because we are created as an image of God. No other creature in the universe (as far as we know) can claim this status, and therefore the responsibility for the fate of the universe falls to us.

To be an "image of God" is to be a created human being. Every single person is an image of God, whether or not they know it or like it. A brief look around our culture tells us that we humans are "image people." The entire advertisement industry is focused on constructing images. Look at the many images in our culture: the intellectual type, the fashion model, the television star, the political pro, the writer, the sports star. Each and all of these images have their appeal and most people focus their lives (whether implicitly or explicitly) on shaping themselves into any one of these images at any given moment. The question we should ask ourselves, however, is why do we seek after images? Why do we always want to be someone else? Or have the look of someone else? Why do we seldom want to be ourselves? And what does it mean to be ourselves? Perhaps we seek after images because we are created to imitate another. In the language of theology, we are created to imitate God because we are created as "image of God." It is a lot easier to imitate a sports star than to imitate God, however. Who knows what God is like? What aspects of God are we supposed to imitate? What does God do for a living?

We see in the life of Francis that one does not have to be a trained theologian to understand the meaning of being "image of God." One simply needs faith in Jesus Christ and belief that we are created as image of God. Francis had a keen insight into the human image when he wrote, "Consider, O human being, in what great excellence the Lord God has placed you, for he created and formed you *to the image* of his beloved Son according to his body and *to his likeness* according to the Spirit."[1] Francis understood that the human person is created in the image of Jesus Christ "according to the body" meaning that the human body is fundamental to being image of God. Then Francis said we are to be like Christ, according to the Spirit. So to be in the image and likeness of God is not simply to have a body but to act, like Christ, in the spirit of love, mercy and compassion. Imagine if we held up Christ as a superstar and wanted to be just like him by the way we look and act in the world. We would not "shop 'til we drop" or glue ourselves to a television all day. We would dress simply and orient our attention toward people instead of things. We would act with compassion, mercy, love, forgiveness, peace and kindness. However, we would not hesitate to get angry with unjust treatment of the poor, with abuse of political power and with religious practices that are empty of content. We would be involved in social, political and economic structures in order to help bring about the reign of God. That is what the Christian vocation is about, following Jesus Christ, the superstar. In our rituals, prayers, practices and beliefs we profess that Christ is our hero and we are his "groupies." We claim to follow him everywhere and want to be like him. At least that is what we say and why we call ourselves "Christians."

Somehow this notion of being a "Christ groupie" has not entirely caught on, even after two thousand years. We still run after images that ultimately lead to dead ends because in them we never find our fulfillment. The great theologian of the Eastern church Gregory of Nyssa once said, "There is nothing remarkable to want to make of man [sic] the image and likeness of the universe; for the earth passes away, the sky changes and all that is contained therein is as transient as the container."[2] That is a more formal way of saying that earthly images evaporate quickly. We may have the image briefly, but after a while it is no longer relevant or meaningful. Nyssa goes on to say that the human's perfection lies not in that which likens him or her to the rest of creation, but in that which distinguishes him or her from the cosmos and likens one to the Creator. Here is the key point. We are not to become *like* what is earthly but something different, something that transcends the earth and transforms it. For where there is likeness or sameness, there can be no real transformation. We are to be distinguished from the creation and likened to the Creator. To be like the Creator, however, to be like God, is to become humble in love. If this is true, then to be an image of God does not separate us from the world but should lead us right into the heart of the matter—literally—the universe, but in a new way, a God-like way, in a way that is transforming.

The classical understanding of the image of God belongs to Saint Augustine. In a deep and penetrating analysis, Augustine likened the human image to the Trinity. If there are three persons in the Trinity, he reasoned, there must be three faculties of the human that enable us to be in relation to God. He described these faculties as memory, intellect and will. Augustine's psychological analysis of the human image is a way of understanding how the human person can know and love God. In a detailed description of the faculties he indicated that memory is the intellectual self-consciousness of the subject which through the act of understanding gives rise to true knowledge the subject has of itself. Memory or self-consciousness is logically anterior to all activity and grasps itself in its activity. It is the basis on which knowledge and will stand out: I am, I know and I will. This self-knowledge is the source of the mind's love of itself. For Augustine we cannot love unless we know and we cannot know unless we are capable of knowledge, just as the Father in knowing himself produces the Son and in loving the Son wills the Holy Spirit.[3] Bonaventure was influenced by Augustine and agreed that there is an eternal light within the human mind that enables us to know God and the things of God. However, Bonaventure moved beyond Augustine to a more authentically Christian image.

It is possible that Bonaventure developed his own idea of image primarily because of the example of Francis' life. As we mentioned earlier, Francis became a "Christ-like" figure through his spirit of compassion and self-giving love. Bonaventure wrote that "true love of Christ transformed the lover [Francis] into his image" so that Francis bore in his flesh "the likeness of the Crucified."[4] In his *Soul's Journey into God* Bonaventure indicates that there is only one true image and that is Christ.[5] We humans are made in the "image of the Image." Christ is the Image, he claimed, because he is the perfect likeness of the Father. Christ, the Image of the Father, fills the potential of the created human image. We tend toward this perfect image but can never become the perfect image itself because we are created.[6] If the meaning of being image of God is Christ and Christ is, in some way, every person, then we would have to admit that to be image of God is not an individual pursuit or an individual vocation so that some people become images of God and others do not because of various factors or circumstances. Rather, if Christ is the image of God and every person is related to

Christ, then to be image of God must mean that all persons are united in the one Christ. The image of God is the unity of persons united in the Person of Christ. The image of God, therefore, does not depend on individual action or prayer or how kind a person is at a given moment in time. The image of God means that humankind is to be united as one, the one Body of Christ: one image, one Christ to the glory of the Father. How to become this one image of Christ is the grace of divinization, that is, to become the likeness of God.

It might be easier to understand divinization by indicating what it is not. It is not necessarily becoming a monk or nun. It does not mean praying all day in one's room or fleeing the world to become holy. It does not mean to be whimsical, eccentric, ethereal or even enlightened. To be divinized means to have the grace of Christ within you, to lay down your life for your neighbor and to wash the feet of the poor. To be divinized is to be like Christ, unafraid to go to the margins and touch the sick, the wounded, the sinners and all those shunned by society. To be divinized is ultimately to live in the spirit of martyrdom, willing to offer up one's life for the sake of the gospel. It is no wonder that we never desire to be divinized because it is easier to follow fleeting earthly images than to risk one's life for a person we really don't know or love someone who cannot repay us in return. Yet, divinization is what lies at the base of our deepest desires. We want to be "like God" only we are unsure of what God we want to be like: the God of Jesus Christ, the god of culture, the god of progress or the god of our own self-centered egos.

The rapid progress of artificial intelligence today indicates that some people want to be like the god of intelligence. They desire an "immortal mind" and will do just about anything from building robots to downloading human neurons into chips to attain this goal. In his book *The Metaphysics of Virtual Reality*, Michael Heim argues that our fascination with computers is more spiritual than utilitarian. It is a way to emulate God's knowledge by bits of information. The cyber world affords human beings a god-like instant access.[7] The inventor Ray Kurzweil's book *The Age of Spiritual Machines*, is an example of just how desperate the human desire to be divinized really is, to the point of sacrificing what is human for the sake of immortality. Kurzweil claims that machine-dependent humans will eventually create the virtual reality of eternal life, possibly by "neurochips" (downloading the human mind into chips) or simply by becoming totally machine dependent.[8] But the humility of God is not about mind, it is about love and what technology cannot do is imitate human love. Love cannot be generated by a machine; it is personal. Only a human person can love another person in a way that is self-transcending. Noreen Herzfeld, a theologian and computer scientist, claims that our pursuit of artificial intelligence is an attempt to make God in our own image. It is a failed pursuit in her view because to be image of God is not a functional operation, it is relational.[9] Jesus did not ask his disciples *what* do you say that I am but *who* do you say that I am. To be an image of God is not to be a an autonomous individual but a person. The Latin word for person, *persona*, is best understood in its root form *per-sonare*, meaning to sound through in one's life. In the person of Jesus Christ, God "sounded through" his life, through his words and actions and ultimately in his act of love on the cross. As the Image of our image, it is Jesus alone who can show us the way to be divinized and from whom comes the grace of divinization.

What does it mean to say that Jesus is our image? How does this speak to us of what we are to strive for or become? Bonaventure reflected on the life of Francis and described the image in which we are created as a harmonious union of body and spirit. Jesus in his humanity had a perfect union of body and spirit. Because of sin, Bonaventure indicated, our bodies have their own inclinations that sometime differ from the desires of the spirit. In the words of Saint Paul, we find ourselves doing one thing and desiring another (Romans 7:14–23). We live with divided selves in search of wholeness. Christ is the truly human one, Bonaventure indicated, and only by living in Christ can one attain a harmony of body and spirit. What does it mean to live in Christ? Does it mean daily prayers? Going to Mass each day? Wearing a cross? We know that a person can do any or all of these things and not really live in Christ. The outer person can be deceptive. To live in Christ requires inward growth. It means first to undergo a change of heart, a desire to leave behind one's sinful attitudes and behaviors and to strive to put on the "mind of Christ." This is what I believe Francis did. He first undertook a life of penance or conversion, and as the desires of his heart slowly changed, so too did his attitudes and behaviors. He began to live with lepers and tend to the sick and outcasts of his society. He renounced material wealth and chose a life of poverty and humility. He and his followers undertook various types of manual labor but received no monetary remuneration for their work. Rather they spoke to their fellow laborers about the things of God and preached the gospel of peace. Long hours of prayer and fasting also helped Francis become more like Christ in his attitudes and actions. Bonaventure wrote that Francis had attained such harmony of being that his body was in harmony with his spirit and his spirit was in harmony with God.[10]

This harmony of being, we might say, is coming to a new level of insight of who we are in relation to God. Christ is the master of contemplative knowledge, Bonaventure claimed, and only by contemplating his divinity and humanity can our minds reach the perfect knowledge of God.[11] To be an image of God, therefore, is not only to become harmonious in body and spirit, like Christ, it is to come to a level of self-knowledge and knowledge of God. In his *Soul's Journey* Bonaventure wrote, "when our mind contemplates in Christ the Son of God, who is the image of the invisible God by nature, our humanity... reaches something perfect."[12] It is interesting here that Bonaventure uses the first person plural to speak of the image of God. When *our* mind contemplates Christ as true God then *we* attain perfect knowledge of God. Each person must make the journey into God but the image depends on every person's efforts.

To come to know Christ as the truth of God among us is the beginning of divinization. As Francis of Assisi deepened his life in Christ, he acquired a spirit of compassionate love that matured into a desire for martyrdom. The life of Christ became so alive in him that he desired to offer up his life, like Christ, to bear witness to the gospel. Bonaventure said that "he [Francis] desired to offer to the Lord / *his own life as a living sacrifice* in the flames of martyrdom / so that he might... / inspire others to divine love."[13] Francis attained a spirit of martyrdom through an enkindling of love. Bonaventure interpreted Francis' desire of crucified love as reaching the highest stage of union with God. Francis had reached such a deep level of union with Christ crucified interiorly that he desired to express this union exteriorly. The lover, according to Bonaventure, desires to be like the Beloved. To be like the Beloved, to become like Christ, in Bonaventure's view, is both an ascent and a descent: an ascent to God in Christ and a descent to where God lives, in one's fellow human beings. Thus, Bonaventure indicated, the more Francis ascended to God the more he descended to his neighbor and to the creatures of the earth. The deeper was his union with God, the deeper was his love of humanity. Francis attained the height of union with God on the mountain of La Verna where he was marked with the wounds of Christ (the stigmata), a visible sign of his union with Christ crucified. After receiving the stigmata, Bonaventure said, Francis was *"fixed with Christ to the cross* / in body and spirit / ...[he] / *thirsted* with Christ crucified / for the multitude of those to be saved....*He burned with a great desire...*to nurse the lepers."[14] While Francis may seem like an exception to the Christian norm of loving God, Bonaventure viewed the stigmatized Francis as a sign for *all* Christians. In a sermon on Saint Francis he wrote, "everyone will have to bear this sign" [the stigmata] as a sign of the mystical body of Christ for as Saint Paul says: *"those who belong to Christ Jesus have crucified the flesh with its passions and desires"* (Galatians 5:24).[15] Why did Bonaventure suggest that all Christians should bear the stigmata? I think he meant that Christian love is not merely a "spiritual experience" but must be visibly expressed in the body. It is one thing to say "I love God," but if someone asked you "would you sacrifice your life out of love of God?" and you said "no," then one might say your love of God is imperfect, maybe even somewhat self-centered. Others might question whether or not you are truly Christian. The type of love that Bonaventure describes—crucified love—is a costly love because it is a burning love. Bernard of Clairvaux described this highest level of love as a pure love of God without limits. "God is the reason for loving God," he wrote, "and the measure of loving him is to love Him without measure."[16] One of the most inspirational martyrs of our time, Archbishop Oscar Romero, lived this spirit of costly love and his words still echo the cry for justice and liberation:

Martyrdom is a grace from God that I do not believe I have
earned. But if God accepts the sacrifice of my life, then may
my blood be the seed of liberty, and a sign of hope that will
soon become a reality. May my death, if it is accepted by
God, be for the liberation of my people, and as a witness of
hope in what is to come. You can tell them, if they succeed
in killing me, that I pardon them, and I bless those who may
carry out the killing.[17]

To arrive at the level of union with God where one has a burning love
of others, to be divinized, is not to withdraw from the world but rather
to become the suffering servant of humanity. Suffering compassion
and the humble descent below oneself is a higher degree of love than
the love by which the soul is absorbed in the furnace of divine love.[18]
Thus to be divinized in the spirit of Christ's love is to pass through
the furnace of suffering in order to come to a level of purified love,
to descend below oneself and to become the humble servant of one's
neighbor. Bonaventure describes this level of love as a "death" by which
one passes over in Christ crucified to the Father. He writes:

Whoever loves this death can see God because it is true
beyond doubt that man will not see me and live. Let us die
and enter into the darkness; let us impose silence upon our
cares, our desires and our imaginings. With Christ crucified
let us pass out of this world to the Father so that when the
Father is shown to us we may say... It is enough for us...
You are the God of my heart, and the God that is my por-
tion forever.[19]

How do we make sense of this "death in Christ"? For Bonaventure we
may say that living in the spirit of crucified love is to live in the dominance of God's grace. It is to have one's heart centered in God and to
find oneself in God. It is, as Beatrice Bruteau points out, to live out of
the spring of spondic (radiant) energy at the core of one's being, an
energy that is in God, with God and for God.[20] To be divinized is to be
free in love in such a way that one is willing to die out of love. Because

of our transformation into God, we love what God loves and his fire of love is our everlasting joy.

But what if we do not make this passage into God? What if we do not pursue the image in which we are created and become the likeness of God, which fulfills our deepest desires? Then, as Thomas Merton points out, all things become our enemies. If we refuse God's love and remain in the coldness of sin and opposition to God and to our fellow human beings, then will God's fire become our everlasting enemy, and love, instead of being our joy, will become our torment and our destruction.[21] Merton writes,

> Hell is where no one has anything in common with any-
> body else except the fact that they all hate one another and
> cannot get away from one another and from themselves.
> They are all thrown together in their fire and each one tries
> to thrust the others away from him with a huge impotent
> hatred. And the reason why they want to be free of one
> another is not so much that they hate what they see in
> others, as that they know others hate what they see in
> them: and all recognize in one another what they detest in
> themselves, selfishness and impotence, agony, terror and
> despair.[22]

Merton's words are frightening and a stark reminder of our bare human-ity—the power of the human person to build up or tear apart, to love or to hate. To speak of Christ, the Living One, as the central principle and organizing energy of the universe is not to overlook the fact that we may either help build up the Body of Christ or we may destroy it. We are called to "put on Christ" so as to have the humble love of God humbly live in us, to be divinized in the spirit of compassionate love. But this life in Christ is not a "feel good," "everyday happy" experience. It is rather as Bonaventure writes, a life in union with the crucified One: "With Christ I am nailed to the cross.... The true worshiper of God and disciple of Christ who desires to conform perfectly to the Savior of all should strive to carry both in one soul's and flesh the cross of Christ."[23]

Yes, there is a cross, which stretches from the inner heart of God to the depths of human darkness. As the cross plunges into the roots of creation's darkness it enters the pain of war, hatred, fear, resistance, violence, abuse, injury, rape, vengeance, terrorism, the cross of every violation of the human spirit that seeks to destroy the goodness of the human person and nature itself. Because the cross begins in the heart of God's overflowing love it brings with it the power of love into the places where humans have failed to image God. We do not see the wisdom of the cross and therefore we fail to grasp the humility of God. But Christ expresses the humble love of God that has descended into the darkness through the cinders of humility in order to draw all men and women to new life. Only when we share the cross with Christ, when we can say "it is no longer I who live but Christ Jesus lives in me," will the cross of the earth be lifted up in the fullness of God's reign. It is *this* love of the crucified and glorified One which is the energy of life in the universe and which helps this incomplete universe move toward its completion in God.

To be an image of Christ who still bears the wounds of human suffering even in glory indicates to us God's continuous involvement in the world and the need for our participation. The wounds of Christ signify that we need a Christian sense of intimacy, to be passionately involved in the lives of people, in the unjust structures of political, social and economic systems, and in the suffering of the world. Only when we are willing to love by way of suffering love will the human wounds of the present be healed in the glory of Christ, and the cross of the world be lifted up into the eternal embrace of the Trinity's love. Christ is not an unrelated intrusion into the universe but the continuation and fulfillment of a long cosmic preparation. All of creation is intended for Christ. "What happened between God and the world in Christ," Hayes writes, "points to the future of the cosmos. It is a future that involves the radical transformation of created reality through the unitive power of God's creative love."[24]

Perhaps we cannot bear the weight of being Christian, of responsibility for our brothers and sisters and for the earth itself. It is easier to live in isolation than to live in relation and strive for true happiness. Yet, the restless human heart rumbles in the universe and there is no peace until it rests in God. It is not creation's fault that we are unable to attain peace. Rather, it was made so by God that we and creation may cry out for God in the pangs of a new birth. We long for the heart of God, to dwell in the ever-swirling dance of the Trinity's infinite love. God extends his heart to us in the person of Jesus Christ. "God co-operates with all those who love him," Paul writes (Romans 8:28). The question is, do we love God and what God do we love? Are we willing to receive the glory of God into ourselves? Are we willing to be divinized? Then and only then can we hope to be the image of God that we are intended to be, the image of the One Christ loving the Father in the Spirit, the unity of all created reality in the unity of God's love. As Jesus prayed, "Father, may they be one in us, / as you are in me and I am in you" (John 17:21).

We are called to be united in the one God of love and will find no rest in the universe until we rest in this love. Christ is the way, the truth and the life and if we are unsure of the way to travel then we have only to look and see the God who is bent over in love for us. We must bend down to see God. We will find him there in the frailty of our humanity, among the poor, the sick, the lame and the blind. Yes, God is there and will always be there until the end of time. For our God is a humble God and faithful in love. He simply needs flesh and blood and a human face to show his goodness. God needs human skin to live in the universe, vessels of passionate love. We have the capacity for God; we are made in God's image. We can be and are called to be co-lovers and co-creators of the universe. We are called to be alive in Christ, the Living One, in whom dwells the promise and future of God.

REFLECTION QUESTIONS

1. How do you see yourself as "image of God"? How do you live out this image?

2. Are you open to the grace of divinization? What does divinization mean to you in today's world?

3. What prevents you from living fully as image of God? What are you willing to sacrifice to allow God's life to shine in you?

NOTES

[1] Francis of Assisi, "Admonition V" in *FA:ED* I, p. 131.

[2] Gregory of Nyssa, "On the Structure of Man," cited in Lossky, *Orthodox Theology*, p. 119.

[3] See Augustine, *The Trinity*, Stephen McKenna, trans. (Washington, D.C.: Catholic University of America Press, 1963); Mary T. Clark, introduction to *Augustine of Hippo: Selected Writings* (New York: Paulist, 1984), pp. 17–21.

[4] Bonaventure, "The Major Legend of Saint Francis," 13.5 in *FA:ED* II, p. 634.

[5] The mystery of Christ the true image is elaborated in Chapter Six of the *Itinerarium* In his *Hexaëmeron* Bonaventure indicates that the Son is the perfect image and expression of the Father, sharing the same nature and thus totally expressing the Father. He writes: "From all eternity the Father begets a Son similar to himself and expresses himself and a likeness similar to himself, and in so doing he expresses the sum total of his potency." See *Hex*. 1.13 (V, 331).

[6] Zachary Hayes, "The Meaning of 'Convenientia' in the Metaphysics of St. Bonaventure," *Franciscan Studies* 34 (1974): 90.

[7] Cited in David F. Noble, *The Religion of Technology: The Divinity of Man and the Spirit of Invention*, second ed. (New York: Random House, 1999), p.159.

[8] For a discussion of artificial intelligence and its implications for Christian life see Ilia Delio, "Artificial Intelligence and Christian Salvation: Compatibility or Competition?" *New Theology Review* (Fall 2003): 39–51.

[9] Noreen Herzfeld, "Creating in Our Own Image: Artificial Intelligence and the Image of God" *Zygon: Journal of Religion and Science* 37 (June 2002): 304. See also Noreen Herzfeld, *In Our Image: Artificial Intelligence and the Human Spirit* (Minneapolis: Augsburg Fortress, 2002).

[10] Bonaventure, "The Major Legend of Saint Francis," 5.9 in *FA:ED* II, p. 567.

[11] This is the theme of Bonaventure's sermon "Christ, the One Teacher of All" in *What Manner of Man?*, pp. 21–55.

[12] Bonaventure, *Itin*. 6.7 (V, 310). Cousins, trans. *Bonaventure*, pp.108–109.

[13] Bonaventure, "The Major Legend of Saint Francis," in *FA:ED* II, p. 600.

[14] Bonaventure, "The Major Legend of Saint Francis," in *FA:ED* II, p. 640.

[15] Bonaventure, "The Evening Sermon on Saint Francis, 1262," in *FA:ED* II, p. 720.

[16] Bernard of Clairvaux, "On Loving God" in *Selected Works: Bernard of Clairvaux*, G.C. Evans, trans. Jean Leclercq, intro., Ewert Cousins, preface (New York: Paulist, 1987), p. 174.

[17] Cited in Mary Catherine Hilkert, *Naming Grace: Preaching and the Sacramental Imagination* (New York: Continuum, 1997), p. 123.

[18] This is Richard of St. Victor's idea of perfect love that was highly influential on Bonaventure. See Ilia Delio, *Crucified Love: Bonaventure's Mysticism of the Crucified Christ* (Quincy, Ill.: Franciscan Press, 1998), pp.127–128.

[19] Bonaventure, *Itin*. 7.6 (V, 312). Cousins, trans. *Bonaventure*, p. 116.

[20] Bruteau, *Grand Option*, pp. 52–54. Bruteau describes "spondic energy" (from the Greek meaning "libation") as "an outpouring…a projection of personal, spiritual, self-existent energy toward and into other persons, and even toward the infrapersonal universe. We will to pour our own life, our own existence, into others that they may be and may be abundantly."

[21] Merton, *New Seeds of Contemplation*, p. 123.

[22] Merton, *New Seeds of Contemplation*, p. 123.

[23] Bonaventure, *Lig. vit.* 1 (VIII, 68). Cousins, trans. *Bonaventure*, p. 119.

[24] Hayes, "Christ, Word of God and Exemplar of Humanity," p. 12.

Conclusion

When Bonaventure penned his words on the humility of God over seven hundred years ago, he had no idea what import they would have for the future of Christian life. Yet, in no other age has the humility of God demanded such attention. We live in an age that struggles with God—the name, the idea, the reality or unreality (depending on our life experience) of God. We struggle with God because we are wired for God and are restless without God. But our Western culture has buried the God of Jesus Christ in a coffin of antiquity and has raised to life new gods—idols of our selfish desires. Slowly but surely our culture of idolatry is collapsing from within. In an article on Teilhard de Chardin and church renewal, Henri de Lubac wrote that "a world which de-Christianizes itself seems to empty itself out from within, first of God, then of the Son of God, then of what he gives of divinity to his Church; and it is usually the surface that collapses last."[1] How can a world empty itself of God from within if not by human consent? And how do humans consent to eradicate God from the world if not by human choice? Isn't it amazing that God has loved us into being to such a degree that he allows us to revolt but never deviates from being faithful in love?

While the world may try to annihilate God, what we see through the lens of Francis and Bonaventure is that the God of humble love is always with us—that is what the Incarnation is about. Jesus Christ is Emmanuel—God with us. What I have tried to show in these chapters is that God is always with us because we are and always have been with God. We emerge out of the infinite love of the Father, Son and Spirit and are, from the beginning, called into the Trinity's cosmic dance of love. In Bonaventure's view, the integral relationship between the Trinity and creation centered in Christ the Word of God, means that we bear within us an openness to receive God into our midst. From all eternity creation has been prepared to receive the fullness of God into it because creation is made for Christ. We humans (and not just Catholics) are created as co-lovers with Christ and are intended to share the fullness of life in God for all eternity. But many of us who call ourselves "Christian" go about the world as if we never heard of Christ or might not really belong to Christ, and we are startled to learn that creation itself is made for Christ—not Christ for creation. We think that Christ saves us *from* the world and we find it hard to believe that Christ saves us *for* the world, that is, Christ heals us of our divisions so that we may be reconcilers and peacemakers for humankind and the earth itself. If Christ is the reason for creation, then we who are Christian should be at the heart of creation, moving it by our actions toward the fullness of Christ. The humility of God is about living in a universe where Christ is the energizing principle, center and goal because in Christ God has humbly bent down and lifted our fragile human nature into unity with divine nature. That is why the humility of God concerns our life as Christians in the universe.

The problem with the God of humble love, as we have (hopefully) seen throughout these chapters, is precisely that God *is* humble, "bent over" in love for a fragile, incomplete creation with obstinate, selfish human beings at its center. If we could let go of our own obsession with what we think is the meaning of it all, we could somehow see the wisdom of God in the playfulness and sometimes messiness of creation. Even in the physical order of nature, God plays and diverts himself in the garden of his creation through chance, disorder and uncertainty. God does not impose rigid control on creation but delights in what is created and allows things to "be." In our world of human suffering, too, we want a "fix-it" God, a God who will vaccinate us against suffering and prevent bad things from happening to good people. It is not that God allows bad things to happen (as if God gives the "OK" signal). Rather, bad things happen despite God's faithful, humble love because creation is finite and contingent and endowed with a finite freedom that can sometimes twist itself into wrong choices. God's love is a compassionate love that embraces human suffering and nature's failures. On the human level suffering can be a means to deeper love and thus a path to wisdom, as Bonaventure realized. It can lead to a level of compassionate love that sees God hidden at the heart of creation. The wise person knows that a God who could love unto death is a God who can heal us of our selfishness and make us whole.

The humility of God is expressed in Christ who has entered the waters of human suffering to bring every person and all creation into the unity of God's love. Unless we stop looking for a God who will lord it over us as a superior or king, we will not know this God of humble love because he is a God who refuses to be superior to his own creatures. The life of Francis shows us that God has chosen to dwell with us in ordinary human flesh—as brother, neighbor, sister and friend. Because God's humility is God's ordinariness, it is the God who Isaiah foretold would be rejected:

> Like a sapling he grew up in front of us,
> like a root in arid ground.
> Without beauty, without majesty (we saw him),
> no looks to attract our eyes;
> a thing despised and rejected by men,
> a man of sorrows and familiar with suffering,
> a man to make people screen their faces;
> he was despised and we took no account of him.
> (Isaiah 53:2–3).

Is this not the God of our culture today, the One who is despised and of whom no one takes account?

It is precisely the dismissal of God today in our culture that makes Christ so important and Christian life a matter of decision. Francis and Bonaventure realized that Incarnation means that God is involved in our world. Jesus Christ expresses God's involved goodness, a God who is so foolishly close that the boundary between divine and human is often blurred. Francis didn't need proofs of God's existence to know God's hidden presence in the world. His own experience of God's goodness and compassionate love for him enabled him to realize God's compassionate love for others as well. Francis opened his eyes to see that the Most High God is humble and hidden in the ordinary, fragile flesh of the human person. We too are to look and see the face of God disguised, wandering as a pilgrim in his own creation. To see is to reveal what is concealed. When we see rightly with the eyes of the heart, we reveal the transcendent presence of God's ultimate goodness in the face of our neighbors, in our brothers and sisters. We discover Christ among us, the Christ who by his death and resurrection is not *a* person but *every* person. We discover that Christ is truly the cosmic Person, the Living One at the heart of the universe. Christ is the God of humble love with a personal face. That is what Francis discovered in the poor and sick, in the lepers and those rejected by society. It is what we are called to discover today, the God of humble love with a personal face, the God bent over in love in the irreproducible uniqueness of the human person, the one who is the nameless face of Christ. As Thomas Merton wrote, "if we believe in the Incarnation of the Son of God, there should be no one on earth in whom we are not prepared to see, in mystery, the presence of Christ."[2] Every single person is essential to the Christ mystery.

That is why we Christians must wake up today and open our eyes to the beauty of this world, to God's involved goodness, to the presence of Christ at the heart of creation. We are to wake up not because we are better than others but because we claim to live in the light and see the truth of God among us. Do we really see the humble presence of God? If so, what do we see and how do we respond to what we see? We cannot claim to see and act as if we are blind. We cannot say "we are Christian" and continue to stand by while Christ is crucified in the poor and oppressed, while Christ is tortured in the victims of war and violence, while Christ dies slowly in those suffering with AIDS, while Christ is rejected for sex, drugs, alcohol, marital infidelity and anything else that drowns Christ in the waters of human deviant behavior. We cannot say we are Christian while the light of the world is rejected for the darkness of humanity. Either we are lying or we really do not know Christ. God's humble love demands our humble response. If we could let go of our selfish desires, our need to control and manipulate and our obsession with knowledge, if we could be attentive to who we encounter and be free to welcome the other into our lives, then we would find God in the ordinary encounters of daily life: a small child, an aging parent, a foreign neighbor, a dying sister, a singing lark, a budding tree, a flower smiling by the side of the road. We could find God's overflowing goodness coursing through the veins of creation, saturating all living things with abundant goodness, a goodness spilling over and inviting us to touch it and share in it. We would see that God is humbly present in every living creature and in all things because God has bent low in love for us, his beloved creation, and we are caught up, as beloved, in the ecstatic love of the Trinity.

We wonder today if it is possible to find God in the world, to see the world in Christ. We cannot make this discovery unless we first make the discovery of God's humble love within ourselves. We cannot know the God of humble love in the diversity of creation unless we know the God of humble love in the inner sanctum of our hearts. We must see first within before we can see without. It is Christ who reveals to us the God of humble love and who teaches us how to become humble in love. When our inner world can welcome a God of humble love; when we can believe that God loves us in our brokenness and incompleteness, our weaknesses and failings, then we can realize that "that which sustains the universe beyond thought and language and that which is at the core of us and struggles for expression is the same thing."[3] The source of the universe and the source of our lives is the same source: the unconditional, surrendered, free love of a humble God. When we find this source in our own lives then we can find this source at the heart of the universe.

It is because the image of God lies deep within each of us that every person can make Christ alive in the world. We have the capacity to bear Christ in our own bodies, to bring Christ to birth, to help move the creation toward its fullness in Christ. We have the capacity, but do we have the will? Bonaventure once said that just as God, in creating the world, created in the human person a potential for beatitude so that the human might freely choose and merit it, he said, so too he created matter lacking its final perfection of form so that it might "cry out" for perfection.[4] By "perfection" he meant the fullness of relationship with God. In his view, the material world is incapable in itself of experiencing the fullness of relationship with God for it is, by its very nature, incapable of any personal relation with God. It is, however, involved in this destiny in and through the destiny of the spiritual creation. Matter is not lifeless and inert. It does not exist to be manipulated, controlled, pillaged or abused. Rather, matter is dynamic and tends toward spirit. It is the human person who stands in the center of creation as a union of matter and spirit, who must lead creation to God. As Zachary Hayes indicates, the destiny of the material cosmos is intertwined with that of humanity.[5] Teilhard de Chardin expressed a similar idea when he said that the universe is in evolution—in Christogenesis—where the consummation of the world and the consummation of God will converge.

Christianity is a religion of evolution toward the fullness of Christ, that is, the universal cosmic Christ who is in person the unity of the reality of God and the reality of the world. Christians are to lead the evolutionary growth toward the fullness of Christ. That is why we are called to be "Christic Christians," to christify the world not simply by our presence but by our actions. We are to be divinized not by making ourselves royal, self-centered kings and queens but by becoming the presence of the Suffering Servant, the compassionate Christ so as to divinize the world. We are to be the sacrament of God's humble love in the world and we are called to bear witness to this love by our lives. Evolution toward Christ requires bonds of compassionate love and we are called to make those bonds of love in the world visible and tangible.

It may be a tremendous burden (or hubris for some) to say that the fate of the universe falls to us, however, if we are Christians it is what we must profess if we believe in the Word made flesh. From a Franciscan perspective such belief means that the whole creation is incarnational because the Word expressed outwardly is God's creation out of Love. The universe gives "voice" to the inner Word of God. As Margaret Pirkl writes: "Every leaf, every cloud, every fruit, every animal, every person, every poor person, every child is to be seen as an outward expression of the Word of God in love. Every creature is sacred because it holds the Word of God, Christ, in a unique way."[6] Merely joining a religious community or going to church on Sunday does not make us Christian nor does it guarantee any higher place in heaven or reduce any unjust punishment we fear we may incur. Christianity is not a system of rules and regulations, it is not a matter of doctrine nor is it about knowledge alone. As Bill Short states, "God did not come as an idea, a message or thought; God came as a baby, a particular baby in a particular place, at a particular time, and God embraces that."[7] God loves to express himself in particular and unique ways and therefore delights in the diversity of creation. To impose sameness or uniformity on any one group of creation is to be ungodly. To deny the diversity of the Christ mystery is to ignore the humility of God.

Christianity is about a living God who is so personal in love that God bends low in love for each and every creature. When we say "I believe in God" we are saying "I believe in God who bends low in love for every person and creature in Christ"—that is why we call ourselves "Christian." Unless we live what we profess then we are something other than Christian. When we spiritualize Christianity and detach it from the human body of human action, when all we are concerned about is who is "right" and who is "wrong," when we raise ourselves up over and against our neighbors or brothers and sisters because of race, color or religion, when we say "we are saved and you are not," then the Body of Christ is reduced to parts, then it becomes fragmented and divided and the whole universe fails to move forward in Christ. Indeed, it begins to fall apart at the seams.

The humility of God is about God but it is also about us. It is about a God who remains faithful amidst the disorder of the world and it is about our ability to love well in a world of chaos. As Christians it is what we are called to do, to love well in a world that is often competitive, self-serving and struggles for survival; to find God at the often messy center of our lives so we can find God hidden in the fragile faces and fragmented spaces of humanity. Francis of Assisi was moved to sympathy for the poor, the marginalized, the damaged and weak in nature, beggars, lepers, the ill, the fish, the water and the rabbit. All reminded him of Jesus. As Pirkl writes, "perhaps better than any

Christian, Francis was aware of the mysterious union that exists among the cosmic, the human and the divine."[8] We, too, are called to find this union in the ordinariness of our lives if we allow ourselves the freedom first to find the Christ center within us, then to follow Christ by trusting in God's unconditional love. We can do it if we enter within ourselves and honestly accept God's humble love for us; if we can say "this is what I am and it is good" and know in that goodness Christ lives. We can do it if we relinquish our idols, our need to control, our frenzied impersonal activity and allow ourselves to enter the still point of our lives wherein lies the seed of eternity. We need the freedom to be ourselves as God has created us and loves us, and we need the courage to live in God's love humbly, attentively and with compassion. If we can do this, then we are free to open our eyes to the wonder of Christ in the marvelous diversity of creation, we are free to celebrate the world in its global richness. When we discover the power of Christ within us we will discover the power to heal the world, and this healing power will be the hope of our future in God.

Notes

[1] Henri de Lubac, "Teilhard de Chardin in the Context of Renewal," *Communio: International Catholic Review* 15 (Fall 1988): p. 361.

[2] Merton, *New Seeds of Contemplation*, p. 296.

[3] Yann Martel, *The Life of Pi* (Orlando, Fla.: Harcourt Books, 2001), p. 48.

[4] Bonaventure II *Sent.* d. 12, a. 1, q. 2, concl. (II, 297). See also Kent Emery, "Reading the Word Rightly and Squarely: Bonaventure's Doctrine of the Cardinal Virtues," *Traditio* 39 (1983): 195.

[5] Hayes, "Christ, Word of God and Exemplar of Humanity," p. 15.

[6] Pirkl, "Christ, the Inspiration and Center of Life," pp. 262–263.

[7] William Short, lecture on "The Good, Good World" cited in Pirkl, "Christ, the Inspiration and Center of Life," p. 264.

[8] Pirkl, "Christ, the Inspiration and Center of Life," p. 265.

Select Bibliography

BOOKS

Bonaventure: The Soul's Journey into God, The Tree of Life, The Life of St. Francis. Introduction and translation by Ewert H. Cousins. New York: Paulist Press, 1978.

Bruteau, Beatrice. *The Grand Option: Personal Transformation and a New Creation.* Notre Dame, Ind.: University of Notre Dame Press, 2001.

Cousins, Ewert H. (ed.). *Bonaventure and the Coincidence of Opposites.* Chicago: Franciscan Herald Press, 1978.

————. *Christ of the 21st Century.* Rockport, Mass.: Element Books, 1992.

————. *Process Theology: Basic Writings.* New York: Newman Press, 1971.

Delio, Ilia. *Crucified Love: Bonaventure's Mysticism of the Crucified Christ.* Quincy, Ill.: Franciscan Press, 1998.

————. *A Franciscan View of Creation: Learning to Live in a Sacramental World.* Vol. 2. *The Franciscan Heritage Series.* Edited by Joseph P. Chinnici. New York: The Franciscan Institute, 2003.

———— *Simply Bonaventure: An Introduction to His Life, Thought, and Writings.* New York: New City Press, 2001.

De Lubac, Henri. *Teilhard de Chardin: The Man and His Meaning.* Translated by René Hague. New York: Hawthorn Books, 1966.

Disputed Questions on the Mystery of the Trinity. Volume III. *Works of Saint Bonaventure.* Introduction and translation by Zachary Hayes. New York: The Franciscan Institute, 1979.

Edwards, Denis. *The God of Evolution.* New York: Paulist Press, 1999.

Fiddes, Paul S. *The Creative Suffering of God.* Oxford: Clarendon Press, 1988.

Francis of Assisi: Early Documents. Volume I. *The Saint.* Edited by Regis J. Armstrong, J.A. Wayne Hellmann and William J. Short. New York: New City Press, 1999.

Francis of Assisi: Early Documents. Volume II. *The Founder.* Edited by Regis J. Armstrong, J.A. Wayne Hellmann, and William J. Short. New York: New City Press, 2000.

Haught, John F. *Science & Religion: From Conflict to Conversation.* New York: Paulist, 1995.

Hayes, Zachary. *The Hidden Center: Spirituality and Speculative Christology in St. Bonaventure.* New York: The Franciscan Institute, 1992.

Herzfeld, Noreen. *In Our Image: Artificial Intelligence and the Human Spirit.* Minneapolis: Augsburg Fortress, 2002.

Maloney, George A. *The Cosmic Christ: From Paul to Teilhard.* New York: Sheed and Ward, 1968.

Marion, Jean-Luc. *God Without Being.* Translated by Thomas A. Carlson. Chicago: University of Chicago Press, 1991.

Matura, Thadée. *Francis of Assisi: The Message in His Writings.* Translated by Paul Barrett. New York: The Franciscan Institute, 1997.

Merton, Thomas. *New Seeds of Contemplation.* New York: New Directions Books, 1961.

Moffatt, Kathleen and Christa Marie Thompson (eds.). *Resource Manual for the Study of Franciscan Christology.* Washington, D.C.: Franciscan Federation TOR, 1998.

Moltmann, Jürgen. *God in Creation: A New Theology of Creation and the Spirit of God.* Translated by Margaret Kohl. Minneapolis: Fortress Press, 1991.

Mooney, Christopher. *Teilhard de Chardin and the Mystery of Christ.* New York: Harper and Row, 1966.

Pancheri, Francis Xavier. *The Universal Primacy of Christ.* Translated by Juniper B. Carol. Front Royal, Va.: Christendom Publications, 1984.

Polkinghorne, John (ed.). *The Work of Love: Creation as Kenosis.* Grand Rapids, Mich.: William B. Eerdmans, 2001.

Teilhard de Chardin, Pierre. *Christianity and Evolution.* Translated by René Hague. New York: Harcourt Brace Jovanovich, 1971.

————. *The Divine Milieu.* Translated by William Collins. New York: Harper and Row Publishers, 1960.

―――――. *How I Believe*. Translated by René Hague. New York: Harper and Row, 1969.

―――――. *The Phenomenon of Man*. Translated by René Hague. New York: Harper Torchbook, 1965.

Volf, Miroslav. *Exclusion & Embrace: A Theological Exploration of Identity, Otherness, and Reconciliation*. Nashville: Abingdon Press, 1996.

Warren, Kathleen A. *Daring to Cross the Threshold: Francis of Assisi Encounters Sultan Malek al-Kamil*. Rochester, Minn.: Sisters of St. Francis, 2003.

What Manner of Man? Sermons on Christ by St. Bonaventure. Translation, introduction and commentary by Zachary Hayes. Chicago: Franciscan Herald Press, 1989.

Wheatley, Margaret J. *Leadership and the New Science: Learning About Organization from an Orderly Universe*. San Francisco, Ca.: Berrett-Koehler Publishers, 1992.

Works of Bonaventure. Translated by José de Vinck. 5 Vols. Paterson, N.J.: St. Anthony Guild Press, 1960–1970.

ARTICLES

Cousins, Ewert H. "Bonaventure and World Religions," in *S. Bonaventura 1274–1974*. Volume III. 696–706. Edited by J.G. Bougerl. Grottaferrata: Collegio S. Bonaventura, 1973.

―――――. "Bonaventure's Christology and Contemporary Ecumenism." In *Maestro di Vita Francescana e di Sapienza Christiana*. Edited by A. Pompei. 343–351. Rome: Pontificia Facoltà Teologica San Bonaventura, 1976.

―――――. "Christ and the Cosmos: Teilhard de Chardin and Bonaventure." *Cord* 16 (1966): 99–105.

―――――. "The Trinity and World Religions," *Journal of Ecumenical Studies* 7.3 (Summer 1970): 476–498.

Danielou, Jean. "The Meaning and Significance of Teilhard de Chardin." *Communion: International Catholic Review* 15 (Fall 1988): 350–360.

Delio, Ilia. "Artificial Intelligence and Christian Salvation: Compatibility or Competition?" *New Theology Review* (November 2003): 39–51.

————. "Does God 'Act' in Creation? A Bonaventurian Response." *Heythrop Journal* 44 (2003): 328–344.

————. "Francis and the Humility of God." *Cord* 51.2 (March/April 2001): 58–69.

————. "Identity and Difference in Bonaventure's *Legenda Maior*." *Studies in Spirituality* 13 (2003): 199–211.

————. "Revisiting the Franciscan Doctrine of Christ." *Theological Studies* 64 (2003): 3–23.

Haught, John F. "Evolution and God's Humility." *Commonweal* 127 (2000): 12–17.

Hayes, Zachary. "Christ, Word of God and Exemplar of Humanity." *Cord* 46.1 (1996): 3–17.

————. "Christology—Cosmology." In *Spirit and Life: A Journal of Contemporary Franciscanism*. Edited by Anthony Carrozzo, Kenneth Himes and Vincent Cushing: 41–58. New York: The Franciscan Institute, 1997.

————. "Incarnation and Creation in the Theology of St. Bonaventure." In *Studies Honoring Ignatius Brady, Friar Minor*. Edited by Romano Stephen Almagno and Conrad L. Harkins, 309–339. New York: The Franciscan Institute, 1976.

Malone, Patrick. "A God Who Gets Foolishly Close." *America* (May 27, 2000): 22–23.

Taylor, Barbara Brown. "Physics and Faith: The Luminous Web." *Christian Century* (June 2–9, 1999): 612–619.

Index